the Power *of* Flour

ROWIE DILLON

the Power of Flour

The deliciously versatile world of flour in baking and cooking

GLUTEN-FREE

✖

For Lynnie. Every day I think of you. I wish you were here to see and read this, and I know you would be so very proud of my creativity.

CONTENTS

INTRODUCTION

There is something in the creative process that creates procrastination and that gets one as anxious as all get-out until everything falls in to place at the eleventh hour. My heart tells me that it's that process of getting what's in your head out that makes and births a book that will be read by many and change a lot of people's thoughts and lives.

When I started my business 15 years ago out of my own curiosity and need, I made a firm decision that Rowie's Cakes was going to be a household name and that I was going to be the queen of gluten-free. The allergy-free and intolerant food on offer was disgraceful; a complete shocker. In my determination to bump the bland out of allergy free, I made it my mission to investigate and experiment with all the gorgeous flours available. I wanted to understand how they work with different recipe methods and applications so I could create food that is completely wicked and delicious, allergic or not.

Gluten-free baking and cooking is not only an art but a science.

Gluten is the rubber band of baking and cooking—it's the rise and fall and the give and pull. Take that out and you have to be able to put it back in, by using different ingredients and methods delivering texture and taste by the bucketload. That's how it is in my world anyway.

The Power of Flour will educate you. I hope it inspires you to get in touch, literally, with your flours.

So, I ask you to get in touch with your flours.

Feel them.

Rub them between your thumb and your forefinger.

Is it squeaky?

Is it soft and powdery or is it gritty and earthy?

Add a little water.

Does it stick together and expand or does it separate or turn to rock?

Embrace your inner professor and become a curious cook.

Be willing to try the grains and flours used here to create pies, cakes, pastries, tarts, breads, salads, dinners and on-the-go treats from scratch.

I love what I do and I hope you will, too.

Rowie

The POWER *of* FLOUR.

The flours, seeds and grains we will cover include:

- Amaranth
- Arrowroot
- Brown rice flour
- Buckwheat
- Coconut flour
- Lupin
- Polenta
- Potato flour

- Potato starch
- Quinoa flour
- Quinoa flake
- Rice flour
- Sorghum
- Tapioca flour
- Teff

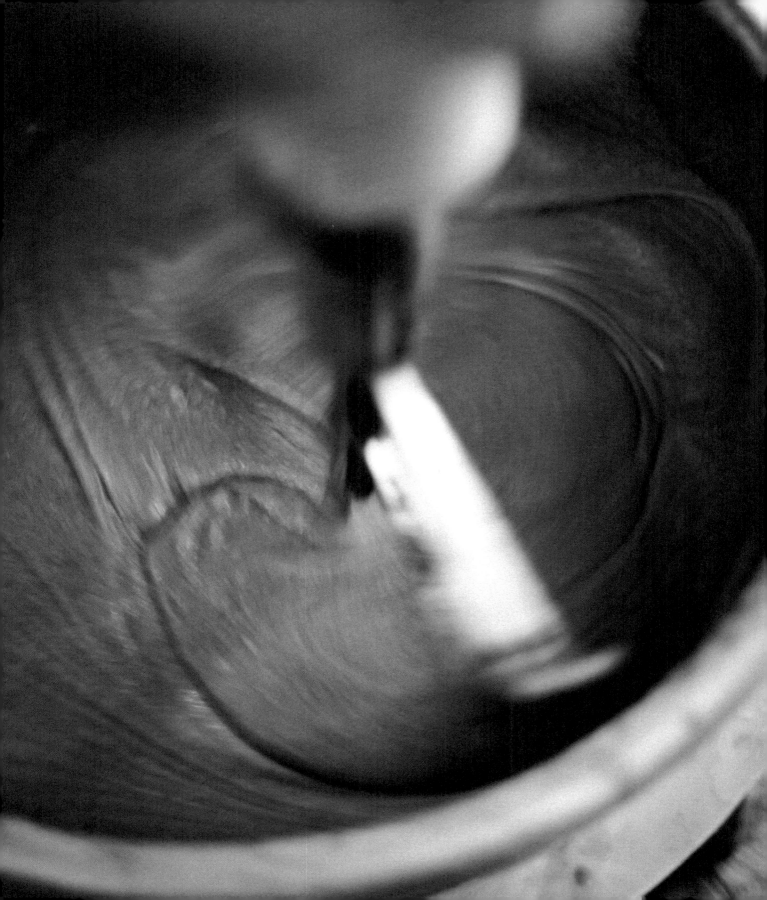

AMARANTH

Amaranth flour is made from the seed of the amaranth plant. It's a leafy vegetable and has a beautiful earthy taste. The grain has been cultivated for more than 8,000 years and it was traditionally used in Aztec religious ceremonies. In my world, amaranth is the cousin to quinoa. Imagine yourself as a teapot: up the top of the mountain is where the quinoa is grown and down the bottom of the mountain is where the amaranth is grown. In simple terms, think about the weather conditions of the bottom of the mountain to understand the properties of amaranth. It is a very absorbent flour and grain. It's a bit like a sponge, gathering up all the water at the bottom of the mountain and collecting it and taking it all in because there's nowhere for the water to run too. Raw amaranth seeds are inedible as they need to be prepared and cooked to create amaranth puff, flour or grain. High in lysine, energy, protein and carbohydrate, as well as having zero sugars, you could say that this ancient grain is a new age superfood. Think of the Aztecs of Mexico and also of the nature of the taste and the source and you will be able to cook and bake your way with this gorgeous, herbacious seed from breakfast through to dinner.

DECADENT GOOEY CHOCOLATE CAKE
Serves 8

More akin to a brownie, this decadent recipe is a perfect pairing with those seasonal berries or fruits that give your cheeks a tingle.

INGREDIENTS
- 230 g (8 oz) *dark (60–65 per cent cacao) chocolate*
- 230 g (8 oz) *unsalted butter, coarsely chopped and softened*
- 290 g (10 oz) *sugar*
- 6 *large eggs*
- 1 tsp *vanilla extract*
- 1 tsp *salt*
- 130 g (4½ oz) *amaranth flour*
- *Cocoa powder or pure confectioners' (icing) sugar, to dust*

METHOD
1. Preheat oven to 180°C (300°F). Lightly grease and line a 20 cm (8 in) springform cake pan.
2. In a medium bowl, melt together the dark chocolate and butter over a saucepan of simmering water, stirring every few seconds until mixture is smooth. Do not let the base of the bowl touch the water. Set aside and allow to cool slightly still on top of the water bath.
3. In a large bowl, use electric beaters to beat the sugar and eggs on medium–high speed until fluffy and double the volume, approximately 3–5 minutes. Beat in the vanilla and salt.
4. Stir in the chocolate mixture, then sift in the amaranth flour and fold it in until the mixture is smooth. Pour into the prepared pan.
5. Bake for 40–45 minutes, until the cake is set and a skewer inserted into the center comes out clean. Allow to cool completely before slicing.
6. You will get a nice cracked finish on top so you may wish to dust your cake with cocoa powder or pure confectioners' (icing) sugar.

The PERFECT AUSSIE ANZAC

Makes 20

These taste so good, you'll be amazed that they are gluten-free. The moment you bite into one you'll be racing back to the bikkie box for seconds!

INGREDIENTS

- 25 g (0.77 oz) puffed amaranth
- 100 g (3½ oz) quinoa flakes
- 45 g (1½ oz) desiccated coconut
- 50 g (1½ oz) toasted flaked almonds (see tip below)
- 75 g (2½ oz) gluten-free plain (all-purpose) flour
- 80 g (3 oz) brown sugar, firmly packed
- 100 g (3½ oz) unsalted butter, melted
- 1 tbsp water
- 115 g (4 oz) honey
- ¾ tsp bicarbonate of soda (baking soda)

METHOD

1. Preheat oven to 180°C (300°F). Line two baking trays with baking paper.
2. Place the amaranth, quinoa flakes, coconut, almond flakes, flour and brown sugar in a large bowl and stir to combine. Set aside.
3. In a medium saucepan, heat the butter, honey and water over medium heat until the butter is melted, stirring continuously. Add the bicarbonate of soda (be quick so you don't lose the fizz), pour into your dry ingredients and stir until well combined.
4. Shape tablespoons of the mixture 3 cm (1 in) apart on your lined trays. Use the back of a fork to flatten slightly.
5. Bake for 12 minutes or until golden. Remove from the oven and set aside to cool. Store in an airtight container for up to one week.

--- TIP ---

To toast the almond flakes, spread the almond flakes on a baking tray and bake at 180°C (300°F) for 3–5 minutes or until golden.

The MOST MAGNIFICENT LOIN *of* LAMB

Serves 6

Amaranth is packed with iron and calcium and has triple the fiber content of wheat. It is a plant and its seed comes off the leaves. We're using amaranth puff here, which is available at most health food stores. Don't just hold yourself to using this stuffing in lamb: think about experimenting with venison or beef. You will become a baked dinner maestro.

INGREDIENTS

- 2 kg, 4¹/₂ pound lamb loin
- sea salt and freshly ground black pepper

Stuffing

- 125 g (4oz) dried apricots, chopped
- 2 celery stalks, finely chopped
- 90 g (30 oz) chopped walnuts

- 40 g (1¹/₂ oz) softened butter
- 1 large white onion, peeled and chopped
- 70 g (27 oz) amaranth puff
- 250 g (8¹/₂ oz) raw chicken livers, chopped,
- 3 rashers rindless bacon, chopped
- 1 tbsp chopped parsley

METHOD

1. Preheat oven to 190°C (370°F). Combine all the stuffing ingredients and spread over the flat part of the lamb. Fold and roll the lamb up and secure with cooking twine.
2. Place the lamb in a baking tray and season all over with salt and pepper. Roast for 1 hour. Rest the lamb, covered in a warm place for 5 minutes.
3. Carve, serve and devour.

ANCIENT GRAIN MUESLI *and* SPRINKLE

Serves 7

This is a week's worth of breakfast or the perfect sprinkle on fruit and yogurt. Once you get into the swing of spending some time on the weekend to prepare for the week ahead, you'll be hooked by how easy, efficient and affordable breakfast can be. Hello sunshine!

INGREDIENTS

- 3 tbsp brown rice puffs
- 3 tbsp pepitas (pumpkin seeds)
- 3 tbsp sunflower seeds
- 75 g (2½ oz) puffed amaranth
- 3 tsp chia seeds
- 1 tbsp goji berries
- 3 tbsp dried mulberries
- 3 tbsp dried strawberries, finely sliced
- 3 tbsp sultanas or raisins
- 3 tbsp dates, pitted, chopped or torn

METHOD

1. Line a baking tray with baking paper. Preheat a grill (broiler) to medium heat. Sprinkle the rice puffs on the prepared tray. Scatter the pepitas and sunflower seeds over the rice puffs and place under the grill (broiler) for 3–5 minutes or until the tops of the rice puffs turn slightly golden.
2. Mix together the remaining ingredients in a large bowl.
3. Add the toasted ingredients, mix well and transfer to an airtight container for up to two weeks.
4. Serve with yogurt, fresh fruit and perhaps a sprinkle of agave nectar or honey. Happy days!

CRISPY FISH TAILS *with* LEMON AIOLI

Serves 4

There's a tale behind every fisherman and his time on the seas bringing fish to the market and to our tables. Here is a superfood—a high protein, crunchy transformation of the ol' fish!

INGREDIENTS

- 2 eggs
- 2 garlic cloves, peeled and crushed
- 1 tsp lemon zest, finely grated
- 1 tsp lime zest, finely grated
- sea salt and freshly ground black pepper
- 170 g (6 oz) amaranth flake
- 800 g (2 lb) skinless snapper fillet, cut into 8 pieces
- olive oil, for frying

METHOD

1. Place the eggs, garlic, lemon and lime zest, salt and pepper in large bowl and whisk to combine.
2. Place the amaranth flake in a separate bowl.
3. Dip a piece of fish into the egg mixture and then into the amaranth flake, and set aside. Repeat with the remaining fish pieces.
4. Heat a good splash of olive oil in a large frying pan over medium heat. Cook your fish in batches, turning over, for 5 minutes or until crisp and golden.

TIP

The Green-Means-Go salad is a great accompaniment to this dish. See the recipe on page 22.

GREEN-MEANS-GO SALAD
Serves 4

Just as crunchy as your fish tails is this slight twist on the ol' 'slaw. I call it my 'Green-Means-Go-Salad' because we're always on the go and this is a fast salad to shred: all you need is a mandolin or a food processor.

INGREDIENTS
- 200 g (7 oz) Chinese cabbage
- 2 Lebanese cucumbers
- 2 salad onions, finely chopped
- 1 tbsp Lemon Aioli (see page 23)
- 2 tbsp cilantro (coriander) leaves

METHOD
1. Using your food processor or mandolin, shred your cabbage then transfer it to a large mixing bowl. Do the same with your cucumber. Finely chop your salad onions and also add to your mixing bowl.
2. Toss the salad with the aioli, transfer to a salad bowl, sprinkle with cilantro to serve.

--- TIP ---

One very easy simple meal that gives you all the power and protein you'll need; it's all in the simplicity.

LEMON AIOLI

Makes 8 fl oz (250 ml)

This delicious, lemony aioli is great with the Crispy Fish Tails with Lemon Aioli (see page 21).

INGREDIENTS

- 1 large egg yolk
- 1 tsp dijon mustard
- 285 ml (9$\frac{1}{2}$ fl oz) extra virgin olive oil
- 285 ml (9$\frac{1}{2}$ fl oz) olive oil
- lemon juice, to taste
- $\frac{1}{2}$ small garlic clove, peeled and crushed
- sea salt and freshly ground black pepper

METHOD

1. Place the egg yolk and mustard in a metal bowl and whisk together. Gradually begin whisking in the oils. Once you've blended one-quarter of the oil you can add the remaining oil in larger quantities.
2. Once the aioli starts to thicken, add your lemon juice to taste. When all the oil is added, add the garlic and season with salt and pepper.
3. If you're feeling zesty you may wish to add some more lemon to taste.
4. Serve in a separate bowl on a grazing platter loaded with your Amaranth Fish and Green-Means-Go Salad.

BURNT ANZAC, ARGENTINIAN CARAMEL *and* CHOCOLATE GANACHE TART

Serves 8–10

This tart is a knockout! That's all I have to say on this one!

_____

INGREDIENTS

- 250 g (9 oz) Anzac cookies (see The Perfect Aussie Anzac on page 16)
- 80 g (3 oz) unsalted butter
- 470 g (16 oz) tinned condensed milk
- 600 g (1lb 3 oz) dark chocolate, chopped
- 235 g (8 oz) thickened cream

METHOD

1. Preheat oven to 180ºC (350ºF).
2. Mix the Anzac cookies in a food processor until they are finely ground. Add in the butter and mix until evenly combined.
3. Remove the mixture and press it into a 35 cm x 11cm (13 in x 4in) loose-based flan tin and place in oven for 15 minutes on 180º C (350ºF). Remove from the oven and set aside to cool in the fridge for 30 minutes.
4. To make the caramel, remove the labels from the unopened cans of condensed milk. Fill a deep, medium saucepan with water and bring it to boil. Carefully place the can in the saucepan, ensuring there is enough water to completely cover the can at all times, topping up water frequently throughout the cooking process.
5. Simmer, uncovered for three hours ensuring the can is completely covered at all time during cooking.
6. Carefully remove the can from the boiling water. Remove the Anzac base mixture from the fridge and allow the caramel to cool completely before opening and spreading on your tart base.
7. To make the ganache, place chocolate in a bowl over a saucepan of simmering water. As you chocolate starts to melt pour in cream and stir consistently until completely melted and combined. Set aside.
8. Pour the chocolate ganache over caramel and place your tart in the fridge for 1 hour or until completely set.
9. Remove from fridge and remove the tart from your flan tin. Grab a splade and serve.

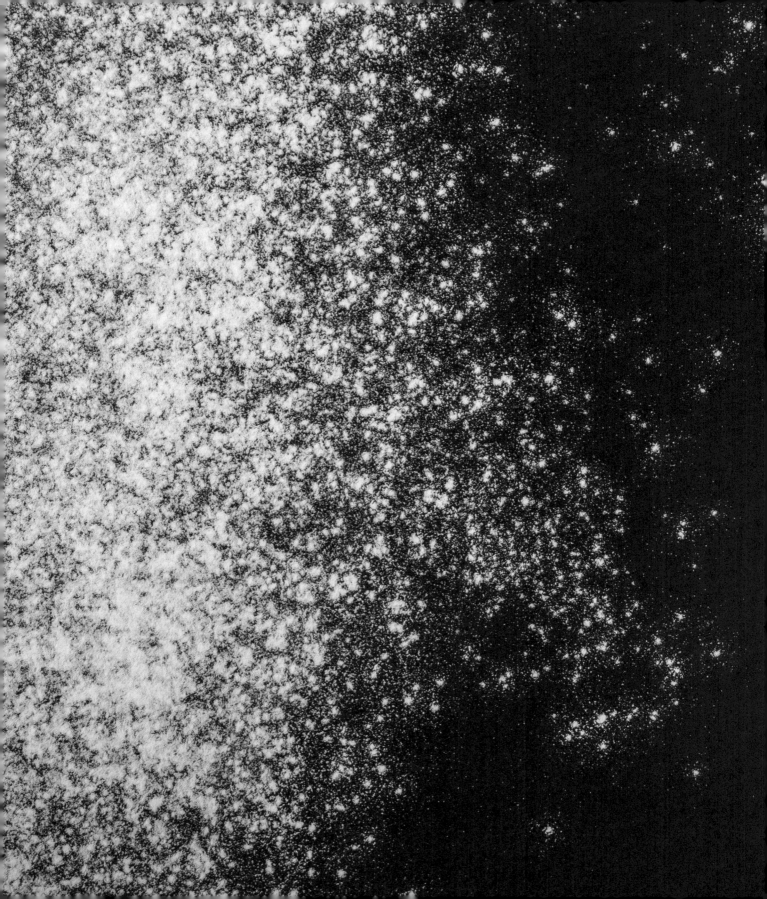

✖

ARROWROOT

I don't want to shock you, but I have to tell you—although arrowroot and tapioca flour are used interchangeably, they are not the same at all. They are both procured from a tropical root vegetable, but are entirely different plants.

Arrowroot starch comes from the maranta arundinacea plant, which is considered a herb. Tapioca is obtained from the cassava root.

Arrowroot is a fine powder ground from the root of the plant. It is tasteless and turns clear when cooked, which makes it ideal for thickening clear sauces and getting a group of flours to work well together. I suggest using it in anything that requires a little "glue". Only add this flour to cold or lukewarm ingredients and gradually increase the heat while stirring frequently (adding directly to hot ingredients will cause it to separate). With its papermaking heritage and wound-healing properties, it's easy to understand why I say it's an awesome glue and more so a friend of other flours, allowing them to come together.

THE BREAD *of* FOUR SEEDS
Makes 1 loaf

Gluten and dairy-free bread is one of those things I receive love letters about. A perfect combination of flour and ingredients, this recipe produces all you could want in terms of taste and texture—and it lasts a few days after baking.

INGREDIENTS

- 300 g (10½ oz) almond meal
- 180 g (6 oz) arrowroot
- 60 g (2 oz) ground flaxseed
- 4 tbsp pepitas (pumpkin seeds)
- 4 tbsp sunflower seeds
- 2 tbsp black chia seeds
- 2 tsp salt
- 1 tsp bicarbonate of soda (baking soda)
- 3 tsp sesame seeds
- 1 tsp poppy seeds
- ½ tsp caraway seeds
- 8 eggs
- 2 tsp apple cider vinegar

METHOD

1. Preheat oven to 180°C (300°F). Grease and line an 11 cm (4 in) x 22 cm (8½ in) loaf tin with baking paper.
2. Combine the almond meal, arrowroot, flaxseed, pepitas, sunflower and chia seeds, salt and bicarbonate of soda in a large bowl. In a separate small bowl combine the sesame, poppy and caraway seeds.
3. Whisk the eggs in a large bowl until foamy. Whisk in the vinegar. Add the almond mixture and stir until combined. Spoon into your prepared tin.
4. Bake for 1 hour or until a skewer inserted into the center comes out clean. Cool on a wire rack and serve in slices to your heart's content.

TIP

A great alternative to ground flaxseed in thish dish is hemp meal.

LIME *and* COCONUT ICE CREAM
Serves 4

I love citrus and coconut. I'd also be dreaming if I thought I'd be able to eat dairy ice cream by the bucketload because I can't. This recipe is dairy-free, gluten-free and easy. If you can't wait for a gorgeous sunny day by the pool or a summer holiday gathering, this is the perfect recipe and the perfect "take me to an island holiday" feeling kind of treat.

INGREDIENTS

Coconut ice cream
- 20 g (0.70 oz) shredded coconut, toasted
- 1¹/₂ tbsp lime zest
- 2 tbsp lime juice
- 55 g (2 oz) coconut flour
- 1 L (33 fl oz) coconut ice cream

Lime syrup
- 110 g (4 oz) superfine (caster) sugar
- 110 ml (3¹/₂ fl oz) water
- 1 large lime, zested
- 110 ml (3¹/₂ fl oz) lime juice
- 1 tsp arrowroot

METHOD
1. Preheat oven to 180°C (300°F). Line a baking tray with baking paper.
2. For the ice cream, sprinkle the coconut evenly over the baking tray and bake for 5 minutes or until the edges are lightly golden. Remove from oven and set aside to cool.
3. Mix the toasted coconut, lime zest, lime juice and coconut flour in a mixing bowl. Place the ice cream in a mixing bowl on your stand mixer.
4. Add your coconut and zest mixture to the ice cream and use the paddle to combine on low speed. Transfer to a container, cover and freeze overnight or until firm.
5. For the syrup, place the sugar and water in a medium saucepan over low heat and stir until the sugar dissolves. Add the zest and simmer for 10 minutes.
6. In a small jug whisk the lime juice and arrowroot until combined. Add to the pan and cook for 2 minutes or until your syrup is just starting to thicken. Chill in the fridge for 3–5 minutes.
7. Serve the ice cream drizzled with the syrup and maybe a Long Island iced tea.

BLUEBERRY PIE
Serves 8

I had a dream about sitting on a picnic rug in Central Park in New York eating this no-bake pie with a silver splade and the love of my life. It was dreamy!

INGREDIENTS

- 250 g (8½ oz) Anzac cookies (see The Perfect Aussie Anzac on page 16)
- 80 g (3 oz) unsalted butter
- 250 g (8½ oz) cream cheese, softened
- 400 g (14 oz) mascarpone
- 2 tbsp coconut sugar (or rapadura panela sugar)
- 80 g (3 oz) good-quality blueberry jam
- 300 g (10 oz) blueberries, plus extra to serve
- 2 tbsp water
- 1 tsp arrowroot

METHOD

1. Whizz the biscuits in a food processor until finely ground. Add the butter and whizz to evenly combine. Press in to a 35 cm (14 in) x 11 cm (4 in) loose-based flan tin and chill in the fridge for 15 minutes or until firm.
2. Beat the cream cheese, mascarpone and 1 tablespoon of the coconut sugar with electric beaters until combined, then spread evenly into the prepared tin. Chill in the fridge for 1 hour or until set.
3. Meanwhile, place the jam, half the blueberries, the remaining coconut sugar and the water in a saucepan over medium heat.
4. Cook stirring for 2-3 minutes or until the berries start to burst, then stir in the arrowroot and remaining berries and cook for a further 30 seconds or until the sauce is thick. Remove from heat and set aside to cool.
5. Remove the pie from your tin, dress with blueberries and serve immediately. Don't forget your splade.

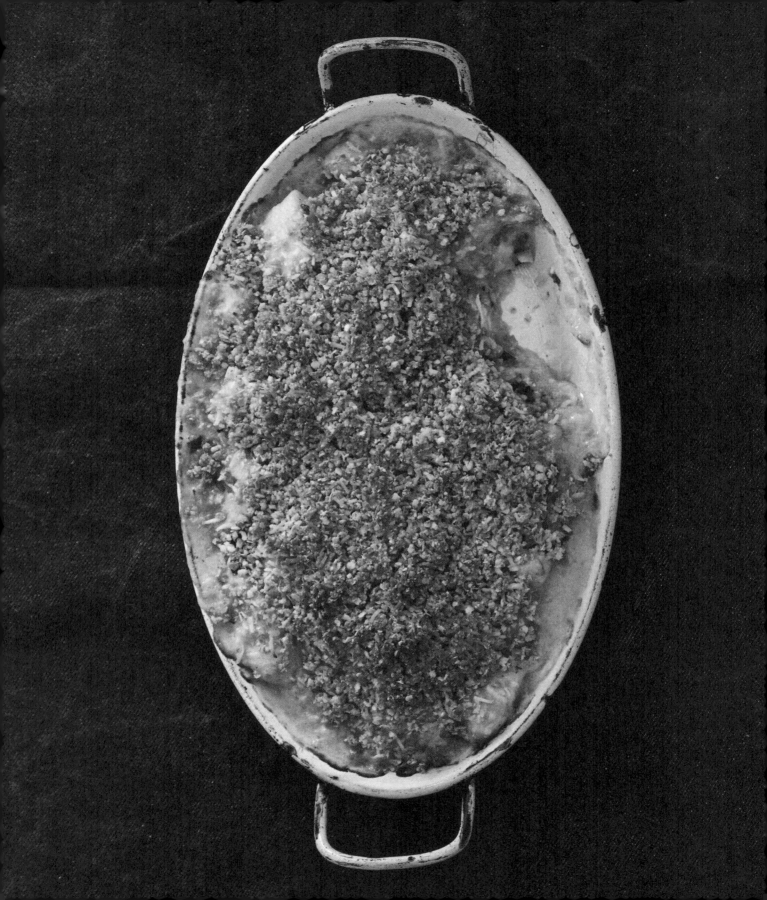

CHICKEN SOUP PIE
Serves 4

Having been a lifelong fan of the pie, there was a not so happy time when I couldn't eat them. But with this ingeniously fun crumbed crust and my gorgeous dairy-free sauce, the Saturday afternoon pie experience is mine again.

INGREDIENTS

Pie filling
- 1.2 kg (2½ lb) skinless chicken breast fillets, diced
- 2 tbsp arrowroot
- sea salt and freshly ground black pepper
- 100 g (3½ oz) dairy-free margarine
- 2 leeks, white part only, halved lengthways and thinly sliced
- 2 tbsp flat-leaf parsley, chopped, plus extra for serving
- 170 ml (5½ fl oz) rice milk
- 250 ml (8½ fl oz) dairy-free plain yogurt
- 1 egg

Crust
- 65 g (2 oz) golden rice flakes
- 30 g (1 oz) shredded coconut
- 75 g (2½ oz) quinoa flakes
- 50 g (1½ oz) dairy-free margarine

METHOD

1. For the crust, combine the rice flakes, coconut and quinoa in a food processer and pulse until the mixture resembles coarse breadcrumbs. (Alternatively, crush with a rolling pin between two sheets of baking paper.) Transfer to a bowl. The crumbs should look rustic and not too fine.

2. Melt the margarine in a frying pan, pour over the crumbs and toss to continue. Set aside.

3. For the filling, preheat oven to 180°C (300°F). Lightly grease four 310 ml (oz) heatproof dishes or a large baking tray.

4. Coat the chicken with the arrowroot and season with salt and pepper. Melt the margarine in a large frying pan over medium–high heat, stir in the leek and fry for 3–5 minutes. Add the chicken and cook for 3 minutes or until the chicken is lightly brown. Remove from the heat and slowly stir in the parsley and rice milk. Return to the heat and simmer, stirring, for 3–5 minutes until the mixture is thick and all the ingredients are combined and well coated.

5. Whisk the yogurt and egg in a small bowl and add to the pan over a medium–low heat with the chicken and leek. Bring to a gentle simmer then remove from heat. Spoon the chicken mixture into the prepared dishes and sprinkle over the reserved crumb mixture. Bake for 25 minutes or until the crumb topping is golden. Serve warm, sprinkled with parsley. Enjoy!

✖

BROWN RICE FLOUR

Brown rice flour is milled from unpolished brown rice that has had the husk removed. It is heavier than white rice flour and has a higher nutritional value. It also has a higher fiber content. If you can close your eyes and imagine you are cooking rice brown rice and you realize how long it takes to cook then you can completely understand why this flour is perfect for baking great biscuits, sweet and savory breads, pancakes and pastry without tasting overly earthy. If you're one for some interesting food chemistry I am sure you will be interested to know that brown rice flour can be combined with vermiculite, which is a mineral that expands when it's heated, for use as a substrate for the growth and bulk cultivation of mushrooms. There you go!

REGAL CRANBERRY *and* PISTACHIO COOKIES
Makes 44

I never thought a cookie would render me silent until I had a moment with my cup of tea and one of these creations.

INGREDIENTS

- 250 g (8½ oz) unsalted butter, chopped and softened
- 125 g (4½ oz) pure confectioners' (icing) sugar, plus extra to serve
- 130 g (4½ oz) buckwheat flour
- 210 g (7½ oz) brown rice flour
- 1 tsp finely grated orange zest
- 75 g (2½ oz) of dried, chopped cranberries
- 55 g (2 oz) chopped unsalted pistachio kernels

METHOD

1. Preheat oven to 170°C (330°F). Line two baking trays with baking paper.
2. Use electric beaters to cream the butter and sugar in a large bowl until pale and fluffy. Add the flours and the zest and beat on low speed until combined. Add the cranberries and pistachios and beat on low until evenly combined.
3. Turn the dough out onto a lightly floured surface and divide into two equal portions. Roll into two 25 cm (10 in) long logs. Cover each log with plastic wrap and refrigerate for 30 minutes.
4. Cut each log into 1 cm (½ in) thick slices and place the rounds 2 cm (¾ in) apart on the prepared trays. Bake for 10–15 minutes until lightly golden. Leave trays on a wire rack to cool completely.
5. Dust delicately and randomly with confectioners' (icing) sugar to serve.

--- TIP ---

You may wish to create bigger biscuits and just roll one larger log as I've done with the batch in the image (left).

The ULTIMATE PIE CRUST

Makes 1 pie crust

The delicate nature of pie making is enhanced with the removal of gluten. Once you understand how to put the give and the take and the push and the pull and rise and fall back into your pastry, pies, or dough, you will have an enlightening experience akin to a lightbulb flash. Then you can start making pastry and pies by the bucketload.

INGREDIENTS

- 85 g (3 oz) sorghum flour
- 40 g (1½ oz) brown rice flour
- 4 tbsp quinoa flakes
- 60 g (2 oz) arrowroot, plus extra for dusting
- 1 tsp psyllium husk
- 1 tsp superfine (caster) sugar
- ½ tsp sea salt
- 115 ml (4 oz) coconut oil, cold, plus extra for greasing
- 3–6 tbsp iced water

METHOD

1. Whisk together all dry the ingredients in a large bowl. Cut the coconut oil into chunks, then add to the dry ingredients. Use your hands or a food processor to rub the oil into the flours until you have a mixture resembling breadcrumbs.
2. Make a well and drizzle in the water 1 tablespoon at a time. Squeeze the dough together—if it crumbles add more water, just a little bit at a time until the dough holds together.
3. Gather the dough together with your hands and shape it in to a flat disc. Loosely wrap in plastic wrap and refrigerate for 30 minutes.
4. Grease a 23 cm (9 in) loose-based flan/pie tin with the extra coconut oil and set aside. Remove the dough from the fridge and roll out in a 28 cm (11 in) circle on baking paper dusted with the extra arrowroot.
5. Place the pastry into the pie dish by sliding or flipping, then shape and trim as desired. Blind bake at 180°C (350°F) lined with pie weights for 15 minutes. Remove from oven and allow to cool.
6. Fill and bake with gorgeous ingredients, either sweet or savory and enjoy.

BROCCOLI, CAULIFLOWER *and* BROWN RICE SALAD

Serves 4

Fiber rich, this salad is loaded with nourishment and packed with taste.

INGREDIENTS

- 300 g (10 oz) brown rice
- 625 ml (22 fl oz) water
- 1 garlic clove, peeled and crushed
- 2 tsp ground cumin
- 2 tbsp peanut oil
- 2 tbsp lemon juice
- 300 g (10 oz), cut in to 1 cm (1/2 in) pieces
- 300 g (10 oz), cut in to 1 cm (1/2 in) pieces
- 4 tbsp brown rice flour
- 120 g (4 oz) pitted green olives, chopped
- 120 g (4 oz) bean sprouts

- 50 g (2 oz) flaked almonds, toasted
- 1 avocado
- handful baby spinach leaves
- small handful alfalfa sprouts
- sea salt and freshly ground black pepper

Dressing:
- 60 ml (2 fl oz) apple cider vinegar
- 1 tbsp honey
- 1 tbsp peanut oil
- 1 red chili, deseeded and finely chopped

METHOD

1. Place the rice and water in a saucepan over high heat. Bring to the boil, cover and reduce heat to low. Cook according to packet directions until almost tender. Remove from heat and set aside, covered, for 10 minutes.
2. Place the garlic, cumin, oil and lemon juice in a frying pan over medium heat. Toss the broccoli and cauliflower in the brown rice flour then add to the pan. Cook, turning with tongs for 3–4 minutes each side.
3. For the dressing, place the vinegar, honey, oil and chili in a small bowl then whisk to combine.
4. Place the cooled rice, olives, bean sprouts, almonds and half the dressing in a bowl and combine. Divide the mixture onto serving plates and top with broccoli, cauliflower, avocado, spinach and sprouts.
5. Drizzle with the remaining dressing and season with salt and pepper to serve.

BROCCOLI, HAM *and* CHEESE PIE
Serves 8

This makes an awesome mid-week meal with a little left over for your lunch box the following day.

___

INGREDIENTS

- 375 g (13 oz) broccoli florets, cut into small, even pieces
- 100 g (3½ oz) sliced leg ham, cut into thick strips
- 100 g (3½ oz) gouda cheese slices, shredded into thick strips
- 1 batch of The Ultimate Pie Crust (see recipe page 42), blind baked
- 250 g (8½ oz) fresh ricotta
- 4 eggs, whisked
- 80 ml (2½ fl oz) milk
- 2 green shallots, chopped
- sea salt and freshly ground black pepper

METHOD

1. Preheat oven to 180ºC (350ºF). Blanch the broccoli in a small saucepan of boiling water for 1–2 minutes. Refresh under cold water and drain well.
2. Place the broccoli, ham and cheese into the blind-baked pastry crust.
3. Place the ricotta, egg, milk, shallots, salt and pepper in a medium bowl and mix until combined. Pour into the pie crust.
4. Bake for 40 minutes or until firm to touch. Serve with a medley of cherry tomatoes and fresh herbs from the garden.

PEA, EGG *and* HAM PIE

Serves 8

Perfect for lunch and an ideal way to give the kids some vegetables in a flavor-packed pastry.

INGREDIENTS

- 2 courgettes (zucchini), thinly sliced
- 1 red pepper (capsicum), cut into 2 cm (³/₄ in) strips
- 1 bunch asparagus, trimmed
- 150 g (5 oz) sliced ham, shredded
- 125 g (4¹/₂ oz) grated tasty cheese
- 4 eggs, whisked

- 2 tbsp shelled peas, fresh or frozen
- 300 g (10¹/₂ oz) light sour cream
- sea salt and freshly ground black pepper
- 1 batch of The Ultimate Pie Crust (see recipe page 42), blind baked

METHOD

1. Preheat oven to 180°C (350°F). Preheat a grill (broiler) on high and grill the courgettes, pepper and asparagus for 2–3 minutes each side, or until tender, then set aside.
2. Layer the ham, cheese and grilled vegetables over the blind-baked pastry crust.
3. Use a whisk to combine the egg, peas and sour cream and season with salt and pepper. Pour the egg and sour cream mixture over the vegetables.
4. Bake for 40 minutes or until firm.
5. Serve with some sprouted greens.

EGG-FREE MUSHROOM *and* PARMESAN PIE

Serves 8

INGREDIENTS

- *40 g (1¹/₂ oz) margarine*
- *250 g (8¹/₂) button mushrooms, thinly sliced*
- *2 green onions, green part only, thinly sliced*
- *4 tbsp cornstarch (cornflour)*
- *340 ml (12 fl oz) milk*
- *2 tbsp finely chives, chopped*

- *4 tbsp grated Parmesan cheese*
- *1 batch of The Ultimate Pie Crust (see recipe page 42), blind baked*
- *100 g (3¹/₂ oz) baby spinach, chopped*
- *fresh watercress, to serve*

METHOD

1. Preheat oven to 180°C (350°F). Melt ¹/₄ of the margarine in a non-stick frying pan over low heat. Add the mushrooms and green onion and cook until the mushrooms have softened then set aside.

2. Melt the remaining margarine in the frying pan over medium heat. Add the cornstarch and cook stirring for 1–2 minutes. Remove from heat, add the milk and stir until smooth. Cook stirring until it thickens. Remove from heat and season with salt and pepper. Stir in half the chives and half the Parmesan.

3. Spoon the mushroom mixture into the blind-baked pie crust. Top with the flour mixture, sprinkle with the baby spinach, remaining Parmesan and chives and bake for 15 minutes or until golden.

4. Serve with fresh watercress.

SWISS ROLL *with* CITRUS CREAM
Serves 6

Possibly one of the easiest, fastest desserts I've ever made. It reminds me of my childhood yet it's far removed from the strawberry jam and white mocha creams I remember. I bet this will be added to your favorites list and you can swap and change your fillings to complement the occasion.

INGREDIENTS

- 110 g (3½ oz) brown rice flour
- 1 tsp gluten-free baking powder
- 110 g (4 oz) golden superfine (caster) sugar (or panela sugar), plus extra for sprinkling
- 50 g (1½ oz) dairy-free margarine
- 2 eggs
- 1 tsp vanilla extract
- pinch of nutmeg

Citrus cream ingredients

- 100 g (4 oz) ricotta
- 250 g (8 oz) spreadable cream cheese
- zest of 1 lime
- zest of 1 lemon
- 1 tbsp golden, superfine (caster) sugar

METHOD

1. Preheat oven to 200°C (390°F). Grease and line a baking tray.
2. Sift the flour and baking powder into a mixing bowl.
3. In a separate bowl, use electric beaters to beat the sugar, margarine and eggs until creamy and smooth. Add the vanilla extract and nutmeg and combine. Fold in the flour on low speed until combined. Spread the mixture evenly into your prepared tray.
4. Bake for 14–15 minutes or until a skewer inserted into the center comes out clean.
5. Meanwhile, for the citrus cream, combine all ingredients and beat until smooth.
6. Remove the Swiss roll from the tin holding the sides of the baking paper and turn it out on to a sheet of baking paper that is sprinkled with panela sugar. Carefully remove the baking paper. Use a sharp knife to trim 2 mm from all around the cake. Cover with a clean, damp cloth and leave for a couple of minutes, then remove the cloth and spread the cake with your citrus cream. Roll gently from the shortest end against you and once you are about to get to the end, slice a diagonal piece off and roll it in a half circle so that the bottom line is underneath. Dust with some more panela sugar and serve. Delectable!

DARK CHOCOLATE *and* RASPBERRY TART

Serves 8

This rich tart is the most indulgent dessert I've ever created. You'll have family and friends clamoring at the door for more. You will need a standing mixer for this recipe.

INGREDIENTS

- 120 g (4 oz) *unsalted butter, softened*
- 125 g (4½ oz) *superfine (caster) sugar*
- 150 g (5 oz) *brown rice flour*
- 50 g (1½ oz) *cocoa powder*

- *pinch of salt*
- 300 ml (10 fl oz) *pouring cream*
- 400 g (14 oz) *good-quality dark chocolate, chopped*
- 250 g (8½ oz) *raspberries*

METHOD

1. Grease the base and sides of a 11 x 34 cm (4 x 13 in) loose-based flan tin. To make the base, put the butter and sugar in the mixing bowl of your stand mixer and beat with the paddle attachment on medium speed for 2 minutes.
2. Sift together the flour, cocoa and salt and gradually add to the butter and sugar mixture until combined.
3. Push the dough into a ball. Roll out the pastry on a lightly floured surface to 3 mm (¼ in) thick.
4. Line the base and sides of the prepared tin with the pastry without trimming. Place in the fridge for 1 hour.
5. Preheat oven to 180°C (350°F). Bake the tart shell for 15 minutes or until crisp then set aside to cool.
6. For the ganache place the cream in a saucepan over medium heat and bring to the boil, then remove from the heat. Place the chocolate in a bowl and pour over the hot cream, stirring until the chocolate is melted and glossy.
7. Spread half the raspberries in an even layer over the tart shell and pour over the ganache. Refrigerate until set.
8. Remove the tart from the tin. Cut with a hot knife and serve with the remaining raspberries.

VEGAN PUMPKIN PIE
Serves 8–10

Sweetened with dates and maple syrup this pie will transport you to sweet pumpkin pie heaven.

INGREDIENTS

- 1½ kg (3½ lb) pumpkin, peeled and coarsely chopped
- 2½ tbsp coconut oil, melted
- 35 g (1 oz) gluten-free cornflour (cornstarch)
- 200 ml (6½ fl oz) coconut milk
- 60 ml (2 fl oz) maple syrup, plus extra to drizzle (optional)
- 1¼ tsp ground cinnamon
- 1¼ tsp mixed spice
- a pinch of salt
- 1 batch of The Ultimate Pie Crust (see recipe page 42), blind baked
- 170 g (9 oz) fresh dates, pitted and chopped
- whipped coconut cream, to serve

METHOD

1. Preheat oven to 180°C (350°F). Roast the pumpkin and coconut oil in a baking dish for 40 minutes until tender. Set aside to cool then process the pumpkin in a food processor until smooth.
2. Whisk the cornstarch and coconut milk in a saucepan over medium heat until smooth. Stir in the pumpkin, maple syrup, cinnamon, mixed spice and salt. Cook, stirring, over medium heat for 8–10 minutes until just boiling and nice and thick. Set aside to cool for 30 minutes.
3. Place the dates evenly in the blind-baked pie crust. Spread the pumpkin and coconut mixture over the top and use a spatula to smooth the surface.
4. Place in the fridge for 4–6 hours until set. Top with whipped coconut cream and a little drizzle of maple syrup if desired.

BUCKWHEAT

Despite its name, buckwheat is not a form of wheat. It is made from the seed of a plant that is related to rhubarb and sorrel. It is not a grass, it's a seed. Once you place buckwheat flour in water it tends to separate into strands. The fruit of the buckwheat plant is similar to the sunflower seed, with a single seed inside a hard outer hull. The seed coat itself is green or tan and this is what gives buckwheat its dark color. Buckwheat noodles are infamous in China and the reason for this is that wheat cannot be grown in their mountain regions. Traditionally, buckwheat noodle dough is pressed to form the noodle. So if you think about the pressing of the dough to extract the water and put the separated strands together you can understand that it would be a great flour to use in pancakes, noodles, pasta and pastry. And for the plonkers, you may not realize that buckwheat is used in distilleries in France and Japan instead of barley.

INCREDIBLE BUCKWHEAT PANCAKES
Serves 5

For me, toppings on pancakes are exciting. It's like having a drawing board to paint taste on, either sweet or savory. You don't need to confine pancakes to breakfast—they are an awesome treat for breakfast, lunch and dinner.

INGREDIENTS

Pancake mix

- 340 g (12 oz) ricotta
- 185 ml (6 fl oz) milk
- 4 eggs, separated
- 130 g (4½ oz) buckwheat flour

- 1 tsp gluten-free baking powder
- 1 tsp gluten-free cocoa powder
- pinch of salt
- 75 g (2½ oz) unsalted butter, softened for greasing

METHOD

1. Place the ricotta, milk and egg yolks in a bowl and stir to combine. Sift the flour, baking powder, cocoa and salt into the ricotta mixture and stir until well combined.
2. Use electric beaters to beat the egg whites in a large bowl until stiff peaks form. Fold the egg whites into the ricotta mixture in two or three batches.
3. Lightly grease a large non-stick frying pan with ⅓ of the butter until foaming. Drop 2 tablespoons of the batter per pancake into the pan and cook, covered, in batches of three over medium heat for 2 minutes until the pancakes are golden on the underside. Turn the pancakes and cook on the other side until golden brown and cooked through. Transfer to a plate and keep warm. Repeat with remaining butter and batter.

TIP

I've served my pancakes with a topping of the Apple and Berry Crumbly. For more delicious pancake topping recipe options, see page 52.

APPLE *and* BERRY CRUMBLY

Serves 10

INGREDIENTS

- 120 g (4 oz) flaked almonds
- 120 g (4 oz) almond meal
- 90 g (3 oz) honey, plus extra to garnish
- 2 tbsp coconut oil
- 1 tsp ground cinnamon

- 1 tsp cocoa powder
- 1 kg (2 lb) green apples, cored and thinly sliced
- 2 tbsp lemon juice
- 2 tbsp honey, for the apples
- 1 vanilla bean, split and scraped

METHOD

1. Preheat oven to 160°C (320°F). For the crumble, place the almonds, almond meal, honey, coconut oil, cinnamon and cocoa in a large mixing bowl and stir to combine.
2. Place the apple, lemon juice and honey and vanilla seeds in a large saucepan and heat and cook over medium heat for about 10 minutes, nurturing your apples with a stir occasionally, until your apple is soft.
3. In a lamington tray, place your apples on the base evenly, including the juice, and sprinkle your crumble on top. Bake for 12–15 minutes or until golden.
4. Evenly cover your pancake with a just over half a cup of crumbly and drizzle with some honey.

SALMON *with* WATERCRESS *and* CASHEWS

Serves 2

INGREDIENTS

- 25 g (0.88 oz) watercress sprigs, plus extra to serve
- 1 garlic clove, peeled
- 115 g (4 oz) toasted cashews, plus extra, chopped, to serve
- 115 g (4 fl oz) coconut yogurt

- 1 tsp finely grated lemon
- 1 tbsp lemon juice
- sea salt and freshly ground black pepper
- 400 g (14 oz) smoked salmon

METHOD

1. Place the watercress, garlic, cashews, yogurt, lemon zest and juice in a food processer and process till smooth. Season with salt and pepper.
2. Liberally spread your pancakes with the watercress and cashew spread. Place one pancake on the other. Curl the salmon on top of the pancakes, dress with watercress sprigs and serve.

SMASHED PEAS *and* PECANS

Serves 2

INGREDIENTS

- 120 g (4 oz) pecans
- 2 tbsp maple syrup
- 450 g (316 oz) shelled fresh peas or frozen peas
- 1 small spring onion, finely chopped
- 1 tbsp finely chopped chervil leaves
- zest and juice of 1 lemon
- olive oil, to serve
- sea salt and white pepper

METHOD

1. Preheat oven to 180°C (300°F). Place the pecans on a baking tray and cover you're the maple syrup. Use your fingers to move the pecans around so there is liberal coverage. Bake for 3–5 minutes or until you have that pecan roasted-nut smell.
2. Bring a medium saucepan of water to the boil over medium heat, add the peas and cook for 3–5 minutes. Drain and cool slightly.
3. In a medium bowl combine the onion and chervil with the lemon zest and juice.
4. In a separate bowl or the saucepan, gently smash the peas with a fork or lightly press with a potato masher—don't turn them into mash, just squash and break them. Add the smashed peas to the onion mixture, toss to combine and finish with a splash of olive oil.
5. For each pancake place a tablespoon of smashing peas in the center—use the back end of the tablespoon to create a dip in your mountain of peas on your pancake. Sprinkle with pecans. Season with salt and pepper and serve.

CHERRY *and* CHOCOLATE

Serves 2

INGREDIENTS

- 415 g (14 oz) cherries; pitted (if cherries aren't in season you can used tinned pitted cherries)
- 400 g (14 oz) dark chocolate

METHOD

1. Melt the chocolate in a heatproof bowl over a saucepan of simmering water.
2. There are two pancakes per serving. Place the first pancake down and dress with cherries and drizzle with a small amount of chocolate. Place the next pancake on top and dress with cherries and any cherry juice and drizzle a little heavier with chocolate. Repeat with remaining ingredients.

✖

The BEST WAFFLES *with* ALMOND BUTTER *and* CHOCOLATE

Makes 5 small waffles

These crisp buckwheat waffles have the most nutty, rich taste and you will love them.

INGREDIENTS

- 200 g (7 oz) buckwheat flour
- 1 tbsp coconut sugar
- 1¼ tsp gluten-free baking powder
- 1 tsp bicarbonate of soda (baking soda)
- ¼ tsp salt
- ¼ tsp ground cinnamon
- 300 ml (10 fl oz) buttermilk
- 4 tbsp melted butter or coconut oil
- 1 large egg
- 100 g (3½ oz) dark chocolate
- 100 g (3½ oz) almond butter

METHOD

1. Preheat a waffle iron. In a medium bowl, whisk together the buckwheat flour, coconut sugar, baking powder, bicarbonate of soda, salt and cinnamon.
2. In another medium bowl whisk together the buttermilk, melted butter and egg.
3. Pour the wet mixture into the dry mixture and stir until there only a few small lumps remaining. Make sure all the liquid is incorporated. Set your batter aside to rest for 5 minutes.
4. Pour the batter into your hot waffle iron and cook until the waffles are barely letting off steam and they are lightly crisp to touch. Repeat with the remaining batter.
5. Melt the chocolate in a heatproof bowl over a saucepan of simmering water (do not let the base of the bowl touch the water).
6. Serve with almond butter and drizzled warm melted chocolate. Yum!

BUCKWHEAT, TURMERIC *and* BEAN SALAD

Serves 4

I call this my green and gold salad. Raw buckwheat prepared and cooked correctly is beautiful and a great change from lettuce, quinoa and rice.

INGREDIENTS

- 210 g (7¹/₂ oz) raw buckwheat
- 100 g (3¹/₂ oz) green beans, trimmed and halved lengthways
- olive oil

- 110 ml (4 fl oz) vegetable stock
- ¹/₂ tsp fresh turmeric, finely grated
- 50 g (1¹/₂ oz) sultanas
- sea salt and freshly ground black pepper

METHOD

1. Soaking the buckwheat overnight in triple the amount of water, drain and rinse really well.
2. Bring a small saucepan of salted water to the boil. Blanch the beans for 3 minutes, drain and run under cold water, then drizzle with a little olive oil.
3. In another saucepan, add the stock and bring to the boil.
4. Add the soaked buckwheat and turmeric and cook for 3–5 minutes, stirring a couple of times until tender. Drain in a colander and place in a large bowl and splash with a little olive oil. Add your beans and sultanas and toss and season and place on a platter or in a serving bowl.

✖

COCONUT FLOUR

Coconut flour fascinates me. It is made from ground coconut meat and has the highest fiber content of any flour, having a very low concentration of digestible carbohydrates, making it an excellent choice for those looking to restrict their carbohydrate intake. It also has a fat content of about 60 per cent.

When I first started working with coconut flour I was amazed at how it zapped up and seized as soon as it came into contact with water. So I bought a whole coconut and I transported myself in my mind to Tahiti where I was with that coconut on its tree. That coconut weathered storms, wind, extreme heat and humidity and also rain and storm conditions and when I cracked that coconut open the liquid inside was cool to drink. So knowing that coconut flour is made of the flesh of the coconut I had to think about how the flesh and the shell incubated to keep the coconut water cool and how the flesh was the second layer of protection after the shell and how it weathered all of that heat and the storms to remain a really good carer of the water and the shell. It then made sense to me that being a protector, of course, the flesh from the coconut made into coconut flour would reject water because it's used to protecting it and it's also used to pushing away rather extreme temperatures. So the easiest way to get the best out of this flour is to use a liquid that is watery but contains a high amount of fat to keep it fluffy.

Since returning from Tahiti I've had a lot of joy baking with coconut flour and getting the layering texture perfect. I hope my story will allow you to experiment with using coconut flour. It's gorgeous!

LIME *and* COCONUT ISLAND CAKES

Serves 8

This is my Islander cake and one of the most famed recipes from my first cookbook. It conjures up images of the Bahamas—big swinging banana leaf fans, rattan armchairs and clear blue water as far as you can see. This is best consumed with a laidback island attitude and a Long Island iced tea.

INGREDIENTS

- 150 g (5 oz) unsalted butter, chopped and softened
- 230 g (8 oz) superfine (caster) sugar
- 5 eggs
- 140 g (5 oz) coconut flour
- 1¹/₂ tsp gluten-free baking powder
- 150 g (5 oz) desiccated coconut
- 430 ml (15 fl oz) buttermilk

Syrup
- 230 g (8 oz) superfine (caster) sugar
- zest and juice of 1 lemon
- zest and juice of 1 lime
- 125 ml (4 fl oz) water

Icing
- 2 egg whites
- 2 tsp lemon juice
- 375 g (13 oz) pure confectioners' (icing) sugar, sifted

METHOD

1. Preheat oven to 175°C(350°F). Grease and line eight dariole moulds or Texan muffin moulds.
2. Use electric beaters to cream the butter and sugar in a large bowl until pale and fluffy. Add the eggs, one at a time, beating well between each addition.
3. Sift the coconut flour and baking powder into a separate bowl and use a whisk to mix in the desiccated coconut.
4. Fold the coconut mixture and the buttermilk into the egg mixture. Pour the batter (it will be very thick) into the prepared moulds or tins and gently smooth over without pushing. Bake for 40 minutes or until firm on top. Cool in the moulds or tins on a wire rack.
5. For the syrup, place all the ingredients in a medium saucepan and bring to the boil over a medium heat, stirring, until the sugar dissolves. Reduce heat to medium-low and simmer for 10–15 minutes without stirring. Drizzle ¹/₃ of the syrup over your moulds or tins. After 5 minutes, drizzle another third of the syrup. If you cakes still need more liquid after another 5 minutes, pour over the remaining syrup, being careful not to add more than the cakes can absorb. Set your cakes aside for at least 3 hours or overnight.
6. For the icing, use electric beaters to beat the egg whites and lemon juice until stiff peaks form. Gradually add the sugar and beat until the icing is thick and holding smooth and shiny "standing" peaks. Be very careful not to overbeat as this will cause the icing to break down into clumps. Remove your cakes from their moulds and use a palette knife to quickly and evenly spread the icing over the cakes, creating peaks over the top and sides.

CHOCOLATE CHUNK BARS
Makes 16

These gorgeous lunch box or morning or afternoon treats are also gluten-free and paleo. You will be amazed at these incredibly easy treats.

INGREDIENTS

- 55 ml (2 fl oz) melted coconut oil
- 70 ml (2½ fl oz) honey or maple syrup
- 2 tsp vanilla extract
- 2 eggs, whisked
- 55 ml (2 fl oz) almond milk

- 8 tbsp coconut flour
- ½ tsp gluten-free baking powder
- ¼ tsp salt
- 85 g (3 oz) dairy-free chocolate, coarsely chopped

METHOD

1. Preheat oven to 180°C (350°F). Grease and line a 16 cm (8 in) baking tray.
2. In a large bowl, whisk together the coconut oil, honey, vanilla, egg and almond milk.
3. In a separate bowl, whisk together the coconut flour, baking powder and salt.
4. Add the dry ingredients to the wet ingredients and mix until smooth. Fold in the chopped chocolate.
5. Bake for 20 minutes or until the edges are golden brown or a skewer inserted comes out clean. Set aside on a wire rack to cool.
6. Cut into squares and enjoy.

The LAMINGTON

Makes 24

The lamington is an Australian dessert that was named after Lord Lamington, the governor of Queensland, Australia in the 1890s. This is a healthy twist an Aussie fave usually consumed in vast quantities.

INGREDIENTS

- 6 eggs
- 1 tbsp vanilla extract
- 2 tbsp honey
- 60 ml (2 fl oz) olive oil
- 70 g (1½ oz) coconut flour

- 2 tsp gluten-free baking powder
- 60 ml (2 fl oz) dairy-free milk (I use almond milk)
- 100 g (3½ oz) dark chocolate
- 75 g (2½ oz) shredded coconut

METHOD

1. Preheat oven to 160°C (320°F). Grease and line a 22 cm (8½ in) lamington tray.
2. Use electric beaters to beat the eggs, vanilla and honey until very light and creamy, approximately 10 minutes. Gradually pour the oil into the egg mixture while beating.
3. In a separate bowl, gently whisk together the coconut flour and baking powder. Fold into the creamed mixture on low speed. Pour the batter (it may be thick) into the prepared tin and smooth over evenly without pushing the batter. Bake for 35 minutes or until a skewer inserted in the middle comes out clean. Set aside to cool completely then cut into 24 squares.
4. Heat the milk in a small saucepan over medium heat until it starts to go frothy on the edges (be careful to not boil). Turn off heat. Add the chocolate and stir until you have a silky chocolate sauce.
5. Cover each side of your little cakes with a light layer of the chocolate sauce.
6. Roll each in the shredded coconut and place on a tray lined with baking paper and leave to set for 5–10 minutes.

CHRISTMAS SHRIMP
Serves 4

I call these Christmas shrimp because they remind me of Christmas and all those gorgeous flavors that mean Christmas to me.

INGREDIENTS
- 12 large green shrimp (prawns), peeled and deveined?
- 55 g (2 oz) coconut flour
- sea salt and freshly ground black pepper
- 1 large ruby red grapefruit
- 70 g (2½ oz) currants
- 2 tbsp maple syrup
- 1 tsp ground wattle seed
- 2 tbsp olive oil

METHOD
1. Preheat oven to 180°C (300°F). Place the shrimp in a plastic freezer bag. Add the coconut flour and shake to coat then season with salt and pepper.
2. Slice the grapefruit into 8–10 slices on the left to right. Place the slices in a medium baking tray to almost cover the base.
3. Sprinkle your currants over the grapefruit and then drizzle your maple syrup liberally to cover the base ingredients.
4. Place the shrimp over the grapefruit and currants but not on top of each other. Sprinkle with the wattle seed and olive oil and bake for 20–25 minutes or until the heads and tails are completely cooked. Cool for 3–5 minutes, then serve.

LUPIN

The legume seeds of lupins, which are beans, were incredibly popular with the Romans.

Lupin is high in protein, dietary fiber and antioxidants. When the flour is ground, the hull of the bean, the so-called skin, is generally removed.

Lupin beans are also sold in jars with a high salt solution— a bit like preserved lemons or pickles—and they can be eaten with their skin on.

Lupin flour has some fermenting properties which makes it perfect for savory recipes or recipes that contain a vegetable, such as a chocolate and beetroot cake as these properties keep the pastry or cake moist and prevent it drying out. The bean itself in salads is an ideal swap for cannellini or borlotti beans.

Enjoy the transformation of a legume into a flour. Happy baking.

CRUNCHY PISTACHIO WAFERS

Serves 8

Best served with a scoop of your favorite ice cream, these little wafers will have you going back and forth to the kitchen for more.

INGREDIENTS

- 2 egg whites
- 8 tbsp superfine (caster) sugar
- 60 g (2 oz) butter), melted and cooled

- 1 tsp vanilla essence
- 8 tbsp lupin flour, sifted
- 8 tbsp raw pistachio kernels, chopped finely

METHOD

1. Preheat oven to 180°C (350°F). Line three baking trays with baking paper.
2. Whisk the egg whites and sugar with a fork until frothy, about 30 seconds. Stir in the butter and vanilla. Fold through the lupin flour to make a batter. Spread the batter thinly over trays to cover baking paper. Sprinkle the pistachios over the batter.
3. Bake one tray at a time for 8–10 minutes or until light golden. Allow to cool completely on trays.
4. Break in to large pieces and store in an airtight container for up to five days.

DEVILISH CHOCOLATE *and* BEETROOT CAKE
Serves 8

INGREDIENTS

- 4 eggs
- 300 g (10 oz) dark chocolate
- 150 g (5 oz) superfine (caster) sugar, plus 150 g (5 oz) extra
- 240 g (8½ oz) grated raw beetroot
- 120 g (4 oz) lupin flour
- 1 tsp gluten-free baking powder
- 1 tbsp cocoa powder, plus extra to serve
- one big spoon to devour it with!

METHOD

1. Preheat to 180ºC (350ºF). Grease and line a high-sided 20 cm (8 in) springform cake tin.
2. Melt the chocolate in a heatproof bowl over a saucepan of simmering water (do not let the base of the bowl touch the water).
3. Grate the beetroot with a grater or a food processor (making sure you have gloves on) and place in a large mixing bowl and make a well. Separate the eggs and place the whites in a mixing bowl. Add the yolk to the beetroot.
4. In a separate bowl, gently use a hand whisk or fork to whisk the 150 g (5 oz) sugar, lupin flour, baking powder and cocoa powder and stir into the melted chocolate. Add the chocolate mixture to your egg and beetroot mix and stir.
5. Use electric beaters to whisk the egg whites on high until you have stiff peaks. Be careful to not overbeat your whites but do make sure you have peaks, as this will create the airiness in your cake as well as the rise as you have no gluten.
6. Use a spatula to fold the egg whites into the beetroot and chocolate mixture until combined.
7. Pour the batter into the prepared pan and bake for 45 minutes or until a skewer inserted into the middle comes out clean. Set aside to cool on a wire rack.
8. Remove the cake from the pan, dust with cocoa and serve.

TOMATO TART

Serves 6–8

There is something very special about a ripe tomato. It makes you want to cook it or eat it.

_____

INGREDIENTS

- 100 g (3¹/₂ oz) lupin flour
- 2¹/₂ tbsp gluten-free cornstarch (cornflour)
- 1 tsp salt
- ¹/₂ tsp gluten-free baking powder
- 125 g (4¹/₂ oz) unsalted butter, chopped and chilled
- 200 g (7 oz) cold mashed potato
- 400 g (14 oz) variety of tomatoes, halved (use a variety of types of tomatoes for the taste and color)
- 3 eggs
- 3 egg yolks
- 250 ml (8¹/₂ fl oz) pouring cream
- ¹/₂ tsp freshly grated nutmeg
- ¹/₂ tbsp chopped dill
- ¹/₂ tbsp chopped flat-leaf parsley
- ¹/₂ tbsp currants
- sea salt and freshly ground black pepper
- extra herbs, to serve

METHOD

1. Preheat oven to 180ºC (350ºF). Lightly grease a 23 cm (9 in) round fluted, loose-based flan tin.
2. Sift the flours into a large bowl and use your hands to mix in the salt, baking powder, butter and potato. Tip out onto a floured surface and knead the pastry, pushing and folding it together for 3 minutes until it comes together in a ball.
3. Roll out the pastry between two sheets of baking paper to make a 30 cm (12 in) circle, dusting as you go. Press into the prepared tin and line the pastry shell with baking paper and pastry weights or uncooked rice. Blind bake for 15 minutes. Cool slightly and remove the baking paper and weights. Reduce oven to 160ºC (230ºF).
4. For the filling, place the halved tomatoes, cut side up, on the baked pastry to cover the entire base.
5. In a separate bowl, whisk together the eggs, egg yolks, cream, nutmeg, dill, parsley and currants. Pour into the pastry case and bake for 25 minutes or until just golden.
6. Season with salt and pepper, garnish with a few extra herbs and serve.

COCONUT *and* PASSIONFRUIT PUDDING
Serves 6

This decadent coconut and passionfruit dessert will warm up any cool day. It reminds me of Nana's Sunday puddings.

INGREDIENTS

- 125 g (4 oz) lupin flour
- ¹/₂ tsp gluten-free baking powder
- 8 tbsp superfine (caster) sugar
- 8 tbsp desiccated coconut
- 160 ml (5¹/₂ fl oz) coconut milk
- 1 egg
- 80 g (2¹/₂ oz) butter, melted and cooled
- pure confectioners' (icing) sugar, to serve

Sauce
- 8 tbsp superfine (caster) sugar
- 3 tsp cornstarch (cornflour)
- 110 ml (4 fl oz) milk
- 2 lemons, juiced
- 3 passionfruit, halved

METHOD

1. Preheat oven to 180°C (350°F). Grease a 1¹/₂ L (52 fl oz) capacity ovenproof dish and place on a baking tray lined with baking paper.
2. Sift the flour and baking powder into a bowl, stir in the sugar and desiccated coconut, then make a well in the center. In a separate bowl whisk together the coconut milk, egg and butter. Pour the mixture into the flour mixture and gently stir to combine. Spoon into the prepared dish and smooth the surface with a spatula.
3. For the sauce, combine sugar and cornstarch in a bowl, then sprinkle over the pudding. Combine the milk and 80 ml (3 fl oz) lemon juice (don't worry if your mixture slightly curdles) in a saucepan and cook stirring over medium heat until the mixture comes to the boil. Remove from heat and stir in passionfruit pulp.
4. Pour the hot lemon and passionfruit mixture over the pudding.
5. Bake for 45–50 minutes or until a skewer inserted into the center of the pudding comes out clean. Dust with pure confectioners' (icing) sugar and serve immediately.

COURGETTE PIZZA *with* PESTO, TOMATO, BASIL *and* RICOTTA

Makes 2

This recipe turns pizza into something that is packed with goodness and loads of nutrition. Low in carbs and high in energy, this is perfect for lunch with friends or even as an afternoon snack or dinner. Your kids will be very happy.

INGREDIENTS

- *6 medium courgettes (zucchini), grated*
- *125 g (4 oz) finely grated Parmesan*
- *1 egg*
- *2 garlic cloves, peeled and crushed*
- *95 g (3 oz) lupin flour*
- *1 tbsp dried or fresh oregano*
- *sea salt and freshly ground black pepper*

- *180 g (6 oz) pesto*
- *250 g (8½ oz) cherry tomatoes, halved*
- *small handful watercress leaves*
- *small handful basil leaves*
- *150 g (5 oz) fresh ricotta*
- *2 tbsp capers*

METHOD

1. Preheat oven to 180°C (350°F). Grease two baking trays and line with baking paper.
2. Place the grated courgette, Parmesan, egg, garlic, lupin flour and oregano in a large mixing bowl and stir to combine. Season with salt and pepper.
3. Divide the mixture between the prepared trays. Bake for 40 minutes or until golden and cooked through.
4. Spread each of the bases with pesto, then top with tomatoes, watercress, basil and ricotta and sprinkle with capers. Serve immediately.

PERFECTLY DELICATE PISTACHIO WAFERS
Makes 12

It's time for lupin to entertain you in a way that you would have never have thought of. This is my gelato and panna cotta accompaniment. And even if you don't have a dessert to be their partner, these delicate jewels are perfect as the ultimate petit four.

INGREDIENTS

- *100 g (3½ oz) unsalted butter, softened*
- *100 g (3½ oz) superfine (caster) sugar*
- *1 egg white*
- *100 g (3½ oz) lupin flour*
- *75 g (2½ oz) ground pistachios*

METHOD

1. Preheat oven to 180°C (350°F). Grease a baking tray and line with baking paper.
2. Use electric beaters to cream the butter and the sugar until smooth. Add the egg white and beat well, then add the lupin flour and mix to combine. Fold in the ground pistachios.
3. You will need to bake these in batches of three at a time. Place 1 tablespoon of the mixture onto your baking tray, then use the back of a spoon to carefully work into a 10 cm (4 in) circle.
4. Bake for 5 minutes or just until the wafer has gently browned. Remove from the oven and allow to cool. Use a palette knife to lift off the tray. Carefully drape over a rolling pin and allow to cool and crisp up. Repeat with the remaining mixture.
5. Store in an airtight container.

✖

POLENTA

Before the introduction of corn, polenta was made from starchy ingredients such as faro, chestnut, millet, spelt and chickpeas. These days polenta is made from corn. When cooked it's wickedly creamy but that depends on the consistency of the grain because you can get fine and course polenta. You can buy instant polenta but in general polenta takes a long time to cook to get that gorgeous creaminess and its best friend is butter. The Italians used to cook polenta in a copper pot known as a paiolo. Over time, polenta has been served as porridge, or baked, fried and grilled. I prefer it creamy, served with beef shin, or a course polenta used in pastry or cakes. Polenta goes fantastically with citrus and it's beautiful with a syrup or served with a gorgeous braise of porcini mushrooms. You don't have to transport yourself to Italy to enjoy polenta—you just need to trust yourself that you have the patience to cook it!

CITRUS *and* PASSIONFRUIT SYRUP CAKES
Makes 12

I am a big fan of citrus. It reminds me of summer and the gorgeous yellowness makes these little cakes and the citrus stand out like stars.

INGREDIENTS

- 160 g (5¹/₂ oz) dairy-free margarine
- 150 g (5 oz) superfine (caster) sugar
- 3 eggs
- 100 g (3¹/₂ oz) polenta
- 2 tsp gluten-free baking powder
- 190 g (6¹/₂ oz) blanched almond meal
- 1 tsp finely lemon zest, grated
- 1 tbsp lemon juice
- 2 tbsp passionfruit pulp

Syrup

- 130 g (4¹/₂ oz) superfine (caster) sugar
- 1 tsp finely grated lemon zest
- juice of 1 lemon
- 2 tbsp water

METHOD

1. Preheat oven to 180ºC (300ºF). Grease a 12-hole muffin pan. (I prefer silicon).
2. Use electric beaters to beat the margarine and sugar until pale and creamy. Add the eggs, one at a time, beating well between each addition.
3. In a separate bowl, use a hand whisk to mix the polenta, baking powder, almond meal and lemon zest. Add to the butter mixture in batches on low speed? until combined. Gently stir in the lemon zest, juice and passionfruit pulp until combined.
4. Spoon the mixture into the prepared pan and bake for 20–25 minutes or until just golden on top or until a skewer inserted in the center of one cake comes out clean.
5. Set aside to cool in the pan on a wire rack until completely cool. Turn out upside down on the wire rack lined with baking paper.
6. For the syrup, combine the sugar, lemon zest, lemon juice and water in a saucepan over medium heat. Cook, stirring, for 5 minutes or until sugar dissolves. Increase heat to high and bring to the boil. Boil without stirring for 3 minutes, then remove from heat.
7. Carefully pour the syrup over the cakes. Set aside to cool then serve.

CREAMY POLENTA
Serves 4

This a basic gorgeous creamy polenta that can be paired with mushrooms and thyme, slow cooked beef shin or oven-baked chicken. The trick to the perfect polenta is two things: the dance of your wrist with the whisk and a good solid-based saucepan.

INGREDIENTS

- *750 ml (25 fl oz) water*
- *170 g (6 oz) polenta*
- *125 ml (4 fl oz) pouring cream (you can use coconut cream)*

- *60 g (2 oz) unsalted butter*
- *sea salt and white pepper*

METHOD

1. In a heavy-based saucepan, bring the water to the boil over a medium heat. Use a good-quality hand whisk to move the water while slowly and gradually adding the polenta until it's completely incorporated. The trick to this is to not be impatient and add the polenta too quickly otherwise it will go lumpy.
2. Reduce heat to low and simmer, stirring with a wooden spoon, for up to 10 minutes until the mixture thickens. Once soft, remove from the heat.
3. Add the cream and butter and stir until well combined. Taste and season with salt and pepper. Serve immediately.

BRAISED MUSHROOMS
Serves 4

These gorgeous braised mushrooms are especially delicious when served with Creamy Polenta. They're an all year round winner!

INGREDIENTS

- 3 tbsp extra virgin olive oil
- 680 g (1½ lb) mixed wild mushrooms or shiitake mushrooms, trimmed
- ½ tbsp marsala (optional)
- 125 ml (4 fl oz) water
- sea salt

METHOD

1. In a large braise pan, heat 1 tablespoon of the olive oil over medium heat. Add ⅓ of the mushrooms, pressing down firmly to sear them. Add the marsala if desired. Transfer to a plate and repeat with the next tablespoon of oil and mushrooms and then repeat again.
2. Return all the mushrooms to the pan, add the water, reduce heat, cover and simmer until tender. Season with salt and serve with creamy polenta (see page 81).

BEEF SHIN

Serves 4

I cooked this for a dinner party once and someone thought I had hired a chef. Beef shin is made from the short osso bucco cut and your butcher will generally laugh when you ask for a 22 cm (8 in) piece of beef shin. Start this recipe just before lunch and at dinner they will all be drooling!

INGREDIENTS

- 80 ml (3 fl oz) of olive oil
- 22 cm (8 in) beef shin
- 100 g (3½ oz) mild pancetta, diced
- ½ onion, peeled and chopped
- 2 garlic cloves, peeled and finely chopped
- 300 ml (10 fl oz) Chinese cooking wine
- 500ml (16 fl oz) veal stock
- 1 tsp finely chopped sage leaves
- Creamy Polenta (see recipe page 80), to serve
- ½ tsp finely chopped thyme, plus extra to serve

METHOD

1. Preheat oven to 150°C (300°F). Heat 1 tablespoon of the olive oil in a large deep-set frying pan over medium heat. Add the beef shin and turn over occasionally until browned, approximately 2 minutes in each position. Transfer to a large casserole dish or Dutch oven.

2. Add the pancetta to the pan and stir over medium heat for 1–2 minutes. Then add the onion and garlic and heat until browned. Deglaze the pan with the Chinese wine and simmer until reduced by half. Transfer to the casserole with the remaining ingredients. Cover and braise in the oven for 2½–3 hours or until the beef shin is meltingly tender.

3. Serve with polenta and a strained jug of the cooking sauce and garnish with thyme.

RICOTTA *and* POLENTA CHIPS *with* THYME SALT
Serves 6

You know when you crave a hot chip but just want a little more? This is it! A really wicked way of making the chip the hero of any dish! Enjoy!

_____

INGREDIENTS

- 1 tbsp sea salt flakes
- 1 tbsp of thyme leaves
- 500 ml (8 fl oz) gluten-free chicken stock
- 170 g (6 oz) instant polenta (or use Creamy Polenta recipe page 80)
- 80 g (3 oz) grated parmesan cheese
- 1 tbsp dairy-free margarine
- handful of rosemary leaves
- sea salt and cracked pepper
- 200 g (7 oz) ricotta
- splash of olive oil, for frying

METHOD

1. To make the thyme salt, place the salt and thyme in a bowl and mix to combine. Set aside.
2. Place the stock in a large saucepan over medium heat and bring to the boil. Gradually add the polenta, whisking continuously for 2–3 minutes. Remove from the heat and stir through the parmesan, margarine, rosemary and salt and pepper. Allow to cool for 10 minutes. Add in the ricotta and fold through to combine.
3. Spoon and press the instant polenta into a lightly greased 20 cm (7.8 in) square cake tin and refrigerate until set. Remove from the tin and slice into thick chips.
4. Heat 1 cm ($1/2$ in) of oil in a large non-stick frying pan over high heat. Add the polenta chips, in batches, and cook for 2–3 minutes each side or until golden. Serve with the thyme salt. Happy days!

POLENTA TAGLIATELLE
Serves 4

For the best results, channel your inner Nonna and knead this pasta firmly. You must have patience and dedication and once you get into the swing of it you will be using this recipe for lasagne, ravioli and the like.

INGREDIENTS

- 250 g (8½ oz) gluten-free cornstarch (cornflour)
- 140 g (5 oz) potato flour
- 300 g (10½ oz) fine polenta, plus extra for dusting
- 3 eggs
- 11 egg yolks
- 185 ml (6 fl oz) soda water

METHOD

1. Sift the flours and polenta into a large bowl. Make a well in the center and add the eggs, gently working them in with your hands. Make another well, add the egg yolks and work them into the mixture, adding a little soda water, 1 tablespoon at a time, until the mixture comes together to form a firm elastic ball.
2. Place the dough on a long sheet of baking paper, lightly dusted with a little of the extra polenta. Knead the pasta firmly with the heal of your hands for 3 minutes. Shape the dough into a log and divide into six portions. Loosely cover portions with plastic wrap. Place one portion of the dough on the floured baking paper, lightly dust the top and use a rolling pin to firmly but gently roll out evenly until 3 mm (⅛ in) thick. Set aside and repeat with the remaining portions of dough.
3. Use a palette or kitchen knife to cut the dough lengthways into 1 cm (½ in) wide strips.
4. Cook immediately in a large saucepan of simmering salted water with a few drops of olive oil in batches (don't overcrowd the pan) for 3–5 minutes, or until al dente. Drain and serve with your favorite pasta sauce—mine is ragu.

✖

POTATO FLOUR *and* POTATO STARCH

Potato flour and potato starch are not the same thing. So knowing the difference is critical when baking gluten-free. The way to remember the difference and understand what you can use either for is by understanding where they come from. Potato flour is made from whole potatoes. The potatoes can be dried or cooked and either way they are dried and ground into flour. Potato flour has a distinct potato flavor and readily absorbs liquid— a little like coconut flour—and its best used in small amounts; combined with other flours. I love it in pastry! On the other hand, potato starch is a very fine white powdery starch, similar in texture to cornstarch (cornflour). Potato starch is made from the dried starch component of peeled potatoes and it has no potato flavor. Potato starch lends a light fluffy, light, airy texture to baked goods and is a great thickener for sauces and custard. When placed in water you will see it go hard. It's fascinating that the little ol' potato can be so varied but so versatile considering it's more than 10,000 years old and had its humble beginnings in Peru.

DELICATE LITTLE SPONGES
Makes 12

I call these my bells of St Clement's. They are feathery, airy and beautiful to look at as well as being the most awesome-tasting little cherubs. I can hear you singing while you bake: "orange and lemons say the bells of St Clement's".

INGREDIENTS

- *350 g (12 oz) superfine (caster) sugar*
- *9 eggs, separated*
- *juice of 1 lemon*
- *200 g (7 oz) potato starch*

Icing
- *500 g (18 oz) pure confectioners' (icing) sugar*
- *zest and juice of 1 lemon*
- *zest and juice of 1 orange*

METHOD

1. Preheat oven to 180°C (350°F). Grease and line 12 high-sided dariole moulds or silicone muffin moulds.
2. Place the sugar, egg yolks and lemon juice in a large mixing bowl and use electric beaters to beat on high speed for 5–8 minutes until the mixture is pale and thick. Sift in the potato starch and gently beat on low speed for 2 minutes.
3. Beat the egg whites in a large mixing bowl until stiff peaks form. Pour the egg yolk mixture into the egg whites and use a spatula to fold in gently, drawing the egg yolk mixture into the egg white mixture until combined. It's very important not to lose the airiness of the egg white.
4. Divide the mixture between the prepared moulds and bake for 30 minutes, until golden on top or when a skewer inserted in to the center comes out clean. Cool in the moulds on a wire rack for 30 minutes, then remove.
5. For the icing, sift the confectioners' sugar into a bowl. Add the lemon and orange zests and juice and stir until smooth. If the icing is too thick, add a tablespoon of water, a few drops at a time until it's the consistency of thickened cream.
6. Ice your individual cakes from the top center using a tablespoon of icing. Pour it on to the top of the cakes and then use the back of a spoon, without touching the cakes, to bring the icing around the sides.

TIP

Gorgeous for a high tea! Any leftovers can be kept in an airtight container for up to five days.

MY VICTORIA SPONGE

Serves 8–10

As I am writing this I am wishing I was in London walking through Fortnum & Mason, looking at all the gorgeous biscuit and tea packaging and then wandering down to the amazing food hall. Six years ago I went in there after an encounter with a Duke on the corner and in all my grace and curiosity knocked over a display of precisely-placed boxed shortbread, sending the staff, dressed in their tails, into a frenzy! But as much as I am very fond of this store, I am even more fond of a perfect sponge with a few fresh berries, a dusting of icing sugar and a nice cup of tea.

INGREDIENTS

- 250 g (8½ oz) unsalted butter, softened
- 250 g (8½ oz) superfine (castor) sugar
- 4 eggs
- zest of 1 lemon
- 250 g (8½ oz) potato starch

- 1 tsp gluten-free baking powder
- 150 ml (5 fl oz) pouring cream
- 1 vanilla bean, split and scraped
- 150 g (5 oz) fresh strawberries, hulled
- confectioners' (icing) sugar, for dusting

METHOD

1. Preheat oven to 190°C (370°F). Grease and line one bundt tin 25cm x 9 cm (9½ x 3½in).
2. Use electric beaters to beat the butter and the sugar until very light and fluffy. Add the eggs, one at a time, beating well between each addition. Add the lemon zest.
3. Sift together the potato starch and baking powder and gradually add to the creamed mixture. Pour the batter into the cake pan and bake for 20–25 minutes or until golden and risen and a skewer inserted into the center of a cake comes out clean.
4. Allow to cool on a wire rack then turn out to decorate.
5. Place the cream, vanilla beans and sugar in a mixing bowl and use electric beaters to beat on high speed until thick. Fold in the strawberries. Place the cream on top of one of the cakes and spread just to the edges with a palette knife or spatula. Allow the cream to gradually fall down the cake, top with strawberries and dust with confectioners' sugar.

The TART OF *all* PICNIC TARTS

Serves 6–8

This tart is spring on its own and it's perfect for a picnic. These lovely ingredients flourish at the edge of winter, reminding us that spring is here and the jonquils are blooming. Happy baking!

INGREDIENTS

- 100 g (3¹/₂ oz) potato flour
- 2¹/₂ tbsp gluten-free cornstarch (cornflour)
- 1 tsp salt
- ¹/₂ tsp gluten-free baking powder
- 125 g (4¹/₂ oz) unsalted butter, chopped and chilled
- 200 g (7 oz) cold mashed potato
- 14 spears asparagus, trimmed and halved from top to bottom, lengthways

- 3 eggs
- 3 egg yolks
- 250 ml (8¹/₂ oz) pouring cream
- 1 tbsp chervil leaves, plus extra to serve
- ¹/₂ tbsp juniper berries
- 100 g (3¹/₂ oz) goat cheese
- sea salt and white pepper

METHOD

1. Preheat oven 180°C (350°F). Lightly grease a 23 cm (9 in) round, fluted, loose-based flan tin.
2. Sift the flours into a large bowl and use your hands to mix in the salt, baking powder, butter and potato. Turn out onto a floured bench and knead the pastry, pushing and folding it together for 3 minutes until pastry comes together in a ball.
3. Roll out the pastry between two sheets of baking paper to make a 30 cm (12 in) circle, dusting as you go. Press into the prepared tin and line the pastry shell with baking paper and pastry weights or uncooked rice. Blind bake for 15 minutes. Cool slightly and remove the baking paper and weights. Reduce oven to 160°C (320°F).
4. To make the filling, place the asparagus on the baked pastry, decorating from the tips from the center to the tail to the side of the tin.
5. In a separate bowl, whisk together the eggs, egg yolks, cream, chervil and juniper berries. Pour into the pastry case.
6. Sprinkle with crumbled goat's cheese and season with salt and pepper.
7. Bake for 25 minutes or until starting to go golden. Season and garnish with a few extra herbs and serve.

PERFECT TEMPURA

Serves 4

The trick to slicing these vegetables thinly is to have a good mandolin.

INGREDIENTS

- 175 g (6 oz) sweet potato, peeled and thinly sliced
- 1 carrot, peeled and thinly sliced lengthways
- 175 g (6 oz) purple potato, peeled and thinly sliced
- 400 g (14 oz) pumpkin, peeled and thinly sliced
- 100 g (3½ oz) green beans, trimmed and halved
- 1 red pepper (capsicum), hull removed and cut in to 2 cm (½ in) strips
- 120 g (4 oz) button mushrooms, cleaned and trimmed

- 300 ml (10 fl oz) soda water
- 70 g (2½ oz) potato flour
- 70 g (2½ oz) potato starch
- ½ tsp gluten-free baking powder
- 1 egg
- sunflower oil, for frying
- tamari, to serve
- sprinkle of sesame seeds

METHOD

1. Refrigerate the vegetables and soda water until cold. Sift the flours and baking powder into a large bowl. Add the egg and cold soda water and whisk to combine.
2. Place the oil in a large saucepan ⅓ of the way up the side. Heat over medium–high heat. Check your oil is ready by dropping in a tiny amount of batter—when it sizzles the oil is ready.
3. Dip the vegetables one at a time into the batter and gently lower into the hot oil.
4. Cook up to four vegetables at a time until the batter is lightly golden. Drain on paper towel. Repeat until all the vegetables are cooked.
5. Serve immediately with tamari dressed with sesame seeds.

FLAT ROCK CHOWDER

Serves 4

Chowder's origin is New England in the USA. I've named this Flat Rock Chowder because flat rock is nearly halfway between New England and New York and I figure this old favorite deserves to travel but be near home. Served with a salted, charred bread and a nice glass of wine, this is the perfect tummy warmer for fall and a great way to show how to thicken with potato flour without any fuss.

INGREDIENTS

- 40 g (1½ oz) butter, chopped
- 200 g (7 oz) rindless bacon, chopped
- 2 celery stalks, finely chopped
- 1 onion, peeled and finely chopped
- 120 ml (4 fl oz) dry white wine
- 1 kg (2½ lb) clams, rinsed
- 750 ml (26 fl oz) chicken stock
- 3 desiree potatoes, quartered and cut into chunks
- 125 ml (4 fl oz) pouring cream

- 1 bay leaf
- 12 scallops
- 2 snapper fillets, skin on, cut into 3–4 cm (1–1½ in) sized pieces
- 100 g (3½ oz) skinned, chopped tomato
- ½ tbsp maple syrup
- 1 tbsp potato flour
- sea salt and freshly ground black pepper
- 2 tbsp flat-leaf parsley, plus extra to garnish

METHOD

1. Melt the butter in a large saucepan over high heat. Add the bacon, celery and onion and cook until tender.
2. In another saucepan, bring the wine to the boil and add the clams, cover and shake for approximately 2–3 minutes.
3. Drain and add the cooking liquid to the bacon mixture and set the clams aside.
4. Bring the bacon and wine mixture to the boil over medium heat, then add the chicken stock, potatoes, cream and bay leaf. Bring to a gentle simmer over low heat until the potatoes start to soften then add the scallops, fish, tomato, maple syrup and sifted potato flour. Stir until it just starts to thicken.
5. Add the clams and parsley and stir gently.
6. Season, garnish with parsley and serve.

CHICKPEA *and* PAPRIKA PATTIES

Serves 4

This recipe is inspired by Jamie Oliver. I love a good patty and what makes this one stand out from the crowd is that it's vegan and scrummy!

INGREDIENTS

- 400 g (14 oz) tinned chickpeas (garbanzo beans), drained and rinsed
- 340 g (11 oz) tinned sweetcorn, drained
- 1/2 bunch fresh cilantro (coriander)
- 1/2 tsp ground paprika
- 1/2 tsp ground cilantro (coriander)
- 1/2 tsp ground cumin
- 1 lemon, zested

- 4 tbsp potato flour, plus extra for dusting
- sunflower oil
- handful of small lettuce leaves
- Cashew and Watercress Spread (recipe page 52)
- 115 g (4 oz) dairy-free cream cheese
- 4 burger buns
- sea salt and freshly ground black pepper

METHOD

1. Place the chickpeas and sweetcorn in the bowl of a food processor. Add half the cilantro leaves, with stalks. Add the spices, zest, potato flour and a pinch of salt and pulse until just combined. Place the mixture in the fridge for 30 minutes to firm up.
2. On a flour-dusted surface, divide and shape the mixture into equal-sized patties.
3. Heat a splash of oil over medium heat in a frying pan. Add the patties and cook until golden and cooked through, turning halfway.
4. Slice your burger buns. Spread a good dollop of on the base. On the top bun spread another good dollop of dairy-free cream cheese. Place a couple of little lettuce leaves on the bottom burger bun and top with your patty.
5. Season with salt and pepper and devour.

QUINOA

Quinoa flour, quinoa grain and quinoa flake—"The gold of the Incas"—that's how many refer to gorgeous quinoa. Eight years ago an organic farmer dropped in to Rowie's Cakes and gave me a bag of quinoa flour and a bag of amaranth flour. I put them aside planning to experiment with them sometime soon. After investigating the properties of quinoa and its spinach and beetroot heritage and the fact that it was a seed and mostly cultivated in Aztec climates, I decided to give the quinoa flour a trial commercially in an egg-free, gluten-free, dairy-free cake. I was converted and the Rowie's 'Eat Me' range was born. The layering texture of the flour delivers a product that is fluffy, tasty, dense and wholesome and I've been using quinoa flour and flake ever since. If you want to put taste and nutrition into gluten-free baking, quinoa flour and flakes are clear winners.

PORRIDGE *with* APPLE, TOASTED COCONUT, GOJI *and* BLUEBERRIES

Serves 2

Kickstart your day with quinoa, one of the most protein-rich foods we know of and therefore an ideal candidate for breakfast. It contains all nine essential amino acids, nearly twice as much fiber as most other grains, it's packed with iron, contains lysine, essential for growth and repair, is awesomely rich in magnesium and contains high riboflavin (b2), which helps to stabilize the metabolism.

INGREDIENTS

- 90 g (3 oz) quinoa, rinsed
- 250 ml (8¹/₂ fl oz) almond milk
- 1 tbsp maple or rice malt syrup
- 1 grated or finely diced apple
- pinch of ground cinnamon

- 2 tsp coconut oil
- 1 tbsp toasted coconut flakes
- ¹/₂ tbsp goji berries
- 1 tbsp blueberries

METHOD

1. In a small saucepan with the lid on bring the quinoa and almond milk to the boil over medium–low heat.
2. Reduce heat to a simmer and add the cinnamon, maple or rice malt syrup, apple and coconut oil.
3. Simmer for 12–15 minutes or until the liquid is absorbed and the quinoa is see through. Remove from heat, add the coconut flakes and berries and serve. Top of the morning to you!

LAYERED COCOA SPONGE *with* QUINOA

Serves 6–8

This cake is a crowd-pleaser and shows the versatility of quinoa flour. There's a secret here: it's all in the method. There's an almost volcanic reaction when the vinegar explodes to create your "egg". It's a bit like dropping bicarbonate of soda into water: it sizzles and holds everything together.

INGREDIENTS

- 195 g (6½ oz) *quinoa flour*
- 40 g (1½ oz) *gluten-free cocoa powder*
- 1 tsp *gluten-free baking powder*
- 230 g (8 oz) *superfine (caster) sugar*
- 125 ml (4 fl oz) *vegetable oil*
- 250 ml (8½ fl oz) *coffee, chilled*
- 2 tsp *vanilla extract*
- 2 tsp *white vinegar*

- **Icing**
- 125 g (4½ oz) *dairy-free margarine*
- 155 g (5½ oz) *pure confectioners' (icing) sugar, plus extra for dusting*
- ½ tbsp *gluten-free cocoa powder*

METHOD

1. Preheat oven to 190°C (375°F). Grease and line two 12 cm (4½ in) cake tins. Mix the quinoa flour, cocoa, baking powder and sugar in a large bowl.
2. Combine the vegetable oil, coffee and vanilla in a separate bowl, then add to the dry ingredients and stir well. Add the vinegar and quickly stir to combine (this is our "egg" and will help the mixture to rise when baked). Don't let the mixture sit. Divide and pour the batter in to the prepared cake tins. Bake for 20–25 minutes or until a skewer inserted in to the middle comes out clean. Cool in the tins then turn out on a wire rack.
3. For the icing, beat the margarine and sugar in a small bowl with electric beaters until well combined. Add the cocoa and beat until well combined and the icing is smooth and thick. Use a palette knife to spread the icing over the top of the base cake. Place your second cake on top.
4. Dust with confectioners' sugar and serve!

--- TIP ---

To cover the top with the butter cream as well, double the icing quantity.

SNACKIE BITES
Makes enough for one large platter

The perfect platter partner. Makes crackers for one large antipasto and cheese platter.
Making these is like weaving a colorful jumper. Once rolled out they look like art in the oven and once they are out of the oven
and broken up and placed on the platter, they will not only enhance your platter offering they will have everyone asking for the
recipe. It's that tinge of Japanese spice with the crunch of the cracker that will elevate your cheese to the next level.

INGREDIENTS

- *30 g (1 oz) black chia seeds*
- *30 g (1 oz) white chia seeds*
- *120 ml (4 fl oz) warm water*
- *50 g (1½ oz) brown rice puffs*

- *35 g (1 oz) quinoa flake*
- *1/3 tsp Japanese spice Shichimi Togarashi*
- *25 ml (5 fl oz) sunflower oil*

METHOD

1. Preheat oven to 200°C (390°F). Combine all the chia seeds with the warm water, stir to combine and set aside.
2. Place all the remaining ingredients except the oil in a large bowl and mix to combine. Add the chia mixture and mix well to combine. Add the oil and mix well to evenly combine.
3. Place the mixture in the center of a piece of baking paper. Place another sheet of baking paper on top, pushing the mixture down slightly. Then, roll it out to a 3 mm (¼ in) thickness.
4. Slide the bottom layer of baking paper with rolled mixture on it onto a large baking tray. Bake for 20 minutes or until crisp.
5. Remove from oven and carefully lift the baking paper with the bites onto a wire rack. Cool completely then break up to place on platter to serve.

QUINOA RISOTTO *with* PEAS, RADISH *and* PECORINO

Serves 4

Although it may look like a grain, quinoa is a seed. It is packed with protein and high in fiber. This light risotto uses quinoa grain. The grain itself is truly versatile and can be used in salads, risottos, porridge, birchers and stuffings. It works with sweet and savory and has no boundaries—all you need to do is think about the meal you want to make and rework it to incorporate quinoa: simple.

INGREDIENTS

- *1 whole garlic bulb*
- *1 tbsp olive oil*
- *1 onion, peeled and finely chopped*
- *285 g (10 oz) white quinoa, rinsed*
- *1 L (2 pints) hot vegetable stock*
- *250 ml (8½ fl oz) water*
- *sea salt and freshly ground black pepper*
- *100 g (3½ oz) pecorino, grated*
- *300 g (10½ oz) green peas, blanched*
- *6 radishes, thinly sliced*
- *1 heaped tbsp chervil, to serve*

METHOD

1. Preheat oven to 200°C (400°F). Wrap the garlic in foil, place on a baking tray and bake for 30 minutes or until softened. Unwrap and allow to cool slightly. Squeeze the garlic out of their skins and into a small bowl, mash and set aside.
2. Heat the oil in a large saucepan over medium heat, add the onion and cook until softened. Add the quinoa and cook for 2 minutes. Add the stock and water, reduce heat to low and cook for 20 minutes, stirring every now and then.
3. Add the mashed garlic, salt and pepper and cook, stirring, for 3 minutes. Add half the pecorino, stir to combine and remove from the heat.
4. Place the quinoa risotto on a platter, season and top with the peas, radishes and chervil.
5. Cover with the remaining pecorino and serve.

The BIG ITALIAN—GNOCCHI *with* BASIL AND TOMATO
Serves 4

My head of bakery, Lorenzo, is Italian. He brings fantastic qualities to my business, he's an adoring father and he loves this recipe. I think he was initially taken aback by the thought of using quinoa flour instead of traditional flour, but after a few batches and a couple of differing flavors he was converted. Thanks Lorenzo for all you do—I am eternally grateful to you for your support and guidance. Grazie.

INGREDIENTS

- *3 sebago potatoes*
- *2 red onions, peel and roughly chopped*
- *1 garlic clove, peeled*
- *olive oil, for drizzling*
- *sea salt and freshly ground black pepper*
- *90 g (3 oz) quinoa flour*
- *1 egg*

- *100 g (3½ oz) grated Parmesan*
- *pinch of nutmeg*
- *6 tbsp butter or dairy-free margarine*
- *115 ml (4 fl oz) tomato passata*
- *handful of pine nuts, toasted*
- *handful basil leaves, torn, plus extra to serve*

METHOD

1. Preheat oven to 180°C (350°F). Grease and line a baking tray. Wash and peel the potatoes and boil in a saucepan of lightly salted water over medium heat until it reaches a boil. Drain and leave to cool, then mash and set aside. Place the onion and garlic in the prepared tray, drizzle generously with oil, season with salt and pepper and bake for 15 minutes or until softened and starting to golden.
2. Place the mashed potato, onion, garlic (remove the skin after roasting), quinoa flour, egg, Parmesan, nutmeg, salt and pepper in a large mixing bowl and mix with your hands until well combined.
3. Form the dough into tablespoonful balls. Bring a large saucepan of salted water to the boil over medium heat.
4. Drop 3–4 gnocchi at a time into the water, lower the heat to a simmer and cook for 3–4 minutes, until the gnocchi rises to the surface. Remove with a slotted spoon and keep warm while you cook the rest of the gnocchi in batches.
5. Melt the butter or margarine in a saucepan over medium heat. Add the tomato passata and a pinch of salt. Cook for 3 minutes until the passata is bubbling. Toss the gnocchi gently through the hot passata and add the toasted pine nuts and basil.
6. Season to taste and serve immediately on a platter garnished with basil.

PORK BELLY STUFFED *with* CHERRIES *and* QUINOA
Serves 6-8

Stuffings are another way to show the remarkable versatility of quinoa flake. I've used this stuffing recipe in chicken and turkey for festive occasions and special dinners. Make sure you have a butcher who will select your pork belly and score it for you. Rolling your stuffed pork belly on your own may be a little frustrating so grab a friend in the kitchen and work together to "twine" it up.

INGREDIENTS

- 1.6 kg (3¹/₅ lb) boneless pork belly, skin scored

Stuffing
- 2 tbsp unsalted butter
- 4 onions, peeled and finely chopped
- 16 celery stalks, finely chopped
- 10 large fresh sage leaves, chopped, or 2 tsp crushed dried sage

- 1¹/₂ L (53 fl oz) chicken stock
- 130 g (4¹/₂ oz) quinoa flake
- 2 tsp salt, plus extra for rubbing
- 4 tsp freshly ground pepper
- 2 bunches flat-leaf parsley, chopped
- 240 g (8 oz) pecans, toasted and chopped (optional)
- 200 g (7 oz) dried cherries (optional)

METHOD

1. Preheat oven to 250°C (480°F). For the stuffing, melt the butter in a large frying pan. Add the onions and celery and cook over medium heat until the onions are translucent, about 10 minutes. Add the sage, stir to combine, and cook for 3–4 minutes. Add 125 ml (4 fl oz) stock and stir well. Cook for about 5 minutes, until liquid has reduced by half.
2. Transfer the onion mixture to a large mixing bowl. Add all the remaining ingredients, including the remaining stock and mix to combine.
3. Place the pork on a work surface, skin-side down, with one long side facing you. Season with salt and pepper and spread with an even layer of stuffing. Roll up the pork to enclose the stuffing. Tie with kitchen twine at 5 cm (2 in) intervals. Rub the pork generously with salt. Transfer to a roasting tray and roast for 15 minutes. Reduce the oven to 180°C (300°F) and roast for 1 hour.
4. Allow to rest for 10–15 minutes, then carve and serve immediately.

SUPER GREEN QUINOA SALAD
with BASIL *and* PISTACHIO

Serves 4

There is no significant difference between red and golden quinoa so don't be frightened that you need to cook them differently. Both offer the same high quality nutrition and nutty, earthy taste. I have a preference for the red, for its color in salads and I find it particularly appealing for its vibrancy and contrast. I've used red quinoa for this recipe because I think the color goes well with all these gorgeous greens.

INGREDIENTS

- *3 large leaves of kale (Tuscan cabbage), ribs removed and finely shredded*
- *small handful fresh basil leaves, chopped*
- *2 tbsp extra virgin olive oil*
- *1–1¹/₂ tbsp fresh lemon juice*
- *¹/₄ tsp sea salt*

- *generous pinch of freshly ground black pepper*
- *185 g (6¹/₂ oz) cooked red quinoa*
- *¹/₂ avocado, peeled and chopped*
- *handful spring greens or sprouts*
- *2 tbsp shelled and lightly chopped pistachios*

METHOD

1. In a large bowl toss together the kale, basil, olive oil, lemon juice, salt and pepper. Massage together for about 3–5 minutes.
2. Add in the cooked quinoa, avocado, spring greens and pistachios, toss together gently and serve.

YUMMY VEGAN BANANA LOAVES
Makes 8

I had a surplus of bananas so I decided to experiment with a vegan banana cake. This recipe makes a super moist cake that will be a hit even if I do say so myself.

INGREDIENTS

- 185 g (6¹/₂ oz) quinoa flour
- 1¹/₂ tsp bicarbonate of soda (baking soda)
- 110 g (4 oz) brown sugar
- ¹/₂ tsp salt
- 4 ripe bananas, plus 1 extra banana, sliced, to top
- 75 ml (3 fl oz) sunflower or canola oil
- 3 tbsp white vinegar
- 125 ml (4 fl oz) water
- 1 tsp vanilla extract
- 1 tsp ground cinnamon
- ¹/₂ tsp ground nutmeg
- sliced banana, for topping

METHOD

1. Preheat oven to 180ºC (300ºF). Grease and line 8 mini loaf tins.
2. In a bowl, stir together the flour, bicarbonate of soda, sugar and salt.
3. In another bowl, mash the bananas with a potato masher or a fork and then add the oil, vinegar, water, vanilla, cinnamon and nutmeg.
4. Add the wet mix to the dry mix in two batches and stir until combined. Pour into prepared tins and dress the center with a thinly sliced piece of banana and bake for 30 minutes or until a skewer in the center comes out clean.

APRICOT *and* CRANBERRY SLICE
Makes 8–10

This is a perfect lunch box hit. It ticks all the nutritional boxes and it's a great way to show you how you can use quinoa flake as well as demonstrate the layering properties of quinoa. It's egg-free too and as easy as punch to make and bake. It's a winner and the house will smell sensational when and after it comes out of the oven.

INGREDIENTS

- 125 g (4¹/₂ oz) *dairy-free margarine*
- 90 g (3 oz) *golden syrup*
- 190 g (3 oz) *quinoa flake*
- 80 g (2¹/₂ oz) *sultanas*
- 65 g (2 oz) *dried cranberries*
- 75 g (2¹/₂ oz) *chopped dried apricots*
- 75 g (2¹/₂ oz) *gluten-free cornstarch (cornflour)*
- 90 g (3 oz) *brown sugar*

METHOD

1. Preheat oven to 180ºC (350ºF). Grease and line a 20 x 30cm (8 x 12 in) baking tray.
2. Place the margarine and golden syrup in a small saucepan over low heat and cook, stirring, until the butter melts.
3. Place the quinoa, sultanas, cranberries, apricots, cornstarch and brown sugar is a mixing bowl and toss well to combine. Make a well and pour the margarine mixture into the bowl.
4. Stir to combine all the ingredients and press into the base of your prepared tin. Bake for 20–25 minutes or until golden. Allow to cool completely in the tin before cutting into slices to serve. Store in an airtight container for up to 1 week.

RICE FLOUR

Rice flour is made from finely milled rice. It is different to rice starch. Rice flour is available in two forms: glutinous and non-glutinous. Glutinous rice is also referred to as sweet rice. Now despite the word "glutinous", neither contains gluten. Non-glutinous rice is generally made from short grain rice and is generally used for confectionery manufacturing. Feel your rice flour and make sure it's fine. It's a perfect swap for most cake and biscuit recipes instead of wheaten flour. Have fun and transport yourself to the paddy fields of Japan and China.

MEYER LEMON PIE
Serves 6

I love using Meyer lemons. They are thought to be a cross between a true lemon and a mandarin or orange. It's so royal in taste that it's often grown as an ornamental tree. Alice Walters rediscovered it in the Californian cuisine revolution at the end of the 1990s. Once you use this tasty creature you won't look back. The scent and taste will drive you wild.

INGREDIENTS

- 115 g (4 oz) white rice flour
- 4 eggs
- 77 ml (2.7 fl oz) freshly squeezed lemon juice
- 227 g (8 fl oz) of honey
- 70 g (2½ oz) shredded coconut
- 1 tbsp vanilla extract
- 340 ml (12 fl oz) almond milk (you can use dairy milk)
- 2 tbsp melted butter
- 250 g (8½ oz) fresh raspberries
- pure confectioners' (icing) sugar or toasted coconut flakes, to serve

METHOD

1. Preheat oven to 180°C (350°F). Grease and line a 23 cm (9 in) springform cake tin.
2. Place all the ingredients in a blender and blend until combined. Pour the mixture into the prepared tin. Bake for 50 minutes or until a skewer inserted into the center comes out clean. Set aside to cool on a wire rack.
3. To serve, dust with confectioners' sugar, coconut flakes or fresh raspberries to serve.

WORLD'S BEST CARROT CAKE
Serves 12

One of my Aunty Leah's best cakes is similar to this one. Leah has inspired me over the years to become a better baker and cook. She's always there to guide and nurture my creative soul. She also just happens to be one mighty, mighty baker.

INGREDIENTS

- 185 g (6½ oz) superfine (caster) sugar
- 2 eggs
- 140 ml (5 fl oz) vegetable oil
- 1 tsp vanilla extract
- 140 g (5 oz) rice flour
- 1 tsp ground cinnamon
- ½ tsp bicarbonate of soda (baking soda)
- ½ tsp gluten-free baking powder
- ¼ tsp salt
- 300 g (10½ oz) shredded carrots
- 55 g (2 oz) roasted chopped walnuts

Icing

- 170 g (6 oz) cream cheese (you can use dairy-free cream cheese), softened
- ³/₄ tsp vanilla extract
- 255 g (9 oz) pure confectioners' (icing) sugar
- 1 tbsp milk
- enough roasted whole walnuts to dress around the edges of your cake

METHOD

1. Preheat oven to 180°C (350°F). Grease and line a 21 cm (8 in) springform cake tin or loaf tin.
2. Use electric beaters to beat the sugar and eggs until pale and fluffy then gradually add the oil and vanilla and beat until smooth.
3. Mix the flour, cinnamon, bicarbonate of soda, baking powder and salt in a bowl. Add to the egg mixture, one cup at a time and beat on low speed until well combined. Add the carrot and roasted walnuts and beat on low speed.
4. Bake for 45 minutes or until a skewer inserted in the center comes out clean. Remove from the oven and cool on a wire rack.
5. For the icing, use electric beaters to beat the cream cheese and vanilla until creamy. Reduce speed to low and beat in the confectioners' (icing) sugar then the milk. Use a palate knife to ice the top first and then the sides of the cake. Decorate with roasted walnuts, carrot and toasted, shredded coconut around the top. Serve immediately.

MELT-IN-YOUR-MOUTH ORANGE SHORTBREAD
Makes 16

Ever wanted to take yourself back to when you used to raid your nana's cookie box? Memories like that inspire me every day to create recipes that fulfil my childhood memories of all things sweet and wonderful. This simple recipe will transport you to those years and will make you think of the tins of shortbread at Christmas. You can bring out your cookie cutters and get the kids to assist, or add a little twist and swap the orange for lemon and lime.

INGREDIENTS

- 250 g (8½ oz) unsalted butter, at room temperature
- 100 g (3½ oz) superfine (caster) sugar
- 300 g (10½ oz) gluten-free plain (all-purpose) flour, sifted
- 90 g (3 oz) rice flour, sifted
- finely grated zest of ½ orange
- 1 tbsp pure confectioners' (icing) sugar, sifted

METHOD

1. Preheat oven to 150°C (300°F). Grease and line two baking trays with baking paper.
2. Use electric beaters to beat the butter and sugar until pale and creamy. Sift your flours together in a bowl and gradually add on low speed until almost combined. Add the orange zest. Use your hands to bring the dough together in a bowl.
3. Turn on to a lightly floured surface and knead until smooth. Divide your dough into two portions. Roll out to 18 cm (7 in) discs and use cookie cutters—whatever shape, size or design—to cut out shapes. Place the shapes on the prepared baking trays, using all the dough.
4. Bake for 40 minutes or until the biscuits are lightly golden (depending on the size of your shapes, your cooking time will vary). Set aside on the trays for 10 minutes to cool before transferring to a wire rack to cool completely.
5. Dust with confectioners' (icing) sugar to serve.

COURGETTE FRITTATA
Serves 8

This is more commonly known as my friendly frittata. A perfect use of rice flour to help bring everything together, this is a crowd pleaser and perfect for a light lunch with friends. Add a crisp salad and a dollop of smoky paprika-infused yogurt with lemon zest and it will be devoured in no time.

INGREDIENTS

- 8 eggs, whisked
- 125 ml (4 fl oz) thickened cream
- 50 g (oz) rice flour
- 2 spring onions (shallots), chopped
- 60 g (2 oz) finely chopped spinach
- handful of mixed herbs such as parsley, chervil and basil
- 120 g (4 oz) courgette (zucchini), shredded
- pinch of smoky paprika
- 60 g (2 oz) crumbed feta
- sea salt and freshly ground black pepper

METHOD

1. Preheat the oven to 180°C (350°F). Grease and line a 21cm (8 in) round pie dish. Lightly whisk the egg, cream and rice flour together. Add the spring onion, spinach, herbs, shredded courgette and paprika in a bowl and toss together.

2. Pour the mixture into the pie dish. Sprinkle the fetta on top and season with salt and pepper.

3. Bake for 25 minutes, or until firm to touch in the center. Didn't I tell you: easy as pie!

SORGHUM

Sorghum is related to sugarcane and to millet and is called "great millet" in some areas of West Africa. Sorghum is a very well-traveled grain that is from the grass plant family. Its long journey commenced thousands of years ago in Africa then continuing along to the Middle East and Asia through ancient trade routes traveling to the colorful Arabian peninsula, then India and China along the Silk Road. It's the fifth most important cereal crop in the world, a powerhouse in nutrition, which is high in protein, iron, fiber and antioxidants. Its digestional attributes make it perfect for those with type 2 diabetes and heart conditions. It has a smooth texture and a mild taste and it's an all-purpose flour, making it wicked to use in sweet breads, bread, cookies and flatbread! At Rowie's Cakes, we use sorghum flour in our bread. We work directly with our grower and miller to ensure we have just the correct thinness of flour that's ground and milled using a traditional stone mill. Once milled its best left to rest for a couple of days before working with it.

The BEST EVER CHOC CHIP COOKIES
Make 16–20

Serve these up to the kids with a glass of milk for afternoon tea and you will be tempted to join them. There is nothing quite like the smell of cookies straight from the oven; it sure does get the tummy rumbling.

INGREDIENTS

- 125 g (4½ oz) unsalted butter
- 40 g (1½ oz) white sugar
- 55 g (2 oz) brown sugar
- 1 egg
- 85 g (3 oz) sorghum flour
- 2 tsp gluten-free baking powder
- 190 g (6 oz) choc chips

METHOD

1. Preheat oven to 160ºC (320ºF). Grease and line two baking trays with baking paper.
2. Use electric beaters to beat the butter and sugars until pale and fluffy. Add the egg and beat for a further 30 seconds.
3. Sift the sorghum flour and baking powder and fold in to creamed mixture on low speed until combined. Add the chocolate chips.
4. Remove the dough from the mixing bowl and roll into a ball. Roll into evenly-sized balls, place on the prepared baking trays and bake for 12–15 minutes or until golden.
5. Place the trays on wire racks to cool and set. I can hear them clambering to the kitchen now!

SALT *and* PEPPER CALAMARI

Serves 4

There's one thing that I love and it's the earthiness that sorghum flour brings to seafood. This batter is extremely versatile; you can use it for courgette flowers, tempura, schnitzel and more.

INGREDIENTS

- 85 g (3 oz) sorghum flour
   tsp salt
- ½ tsp gluten-free baking powder
- 3½ tsp sea salt
- 3½ tsp Szechuan pepper

- 250 ml (8½ fl oz) soda water or gluten-free beer for a beer batter, chilled
- sunflower oil, for frying
- 800 g (28 oz) clean baby squid hoods, cut into rings

METHOD

1. Sift the dry ingredients into a large bowl then slowly drizzle in the soda water. It will bubble and foam up. Mix well with a spoon until it resembles runny porridge.
2. Heat the oil in a large saucepan over medium–high heat and when really hot, coat the squid in the batter and quickly place in the hot oil. Cook in batches for 2–3 minutes at a time until golden.
3. Drain on paper towel and serve immediately.

ARTISAN BREAD

Makes 1 loaf

Bread is a very big sore point for those who are on a gluten-free diet. Well, put those worries away and transport yourself into bakery heaven with a recipe that delivers artisan bread and bread flavors in bucketloads. You will be in heaven.

INGREDIENTS

- *300 g (10½ oz) brown rice flour*
- *220 g (7½ oz) sorghum flour*
- *380 g (13½ oz) tapioca flour*
- *2 tbsp instant yeast*
- *1 tbsp sea salt*
- *2 tbsp xanthum gum*

- *4 eggs*
- *670 ml (22½ fl oz) lukewarm water*
- *65 ml (2 fl oz) grapeseed oil*
- *2 tbsp honey*
- *polenta, to dust*

METHOD

1. Place all the dry ingredients in a mixing bowl and mix on low speed until combined. Place all the wet ingredients into a mixing bowl and whisk together. Pour the wet ingredients into the dry and use a wooden spoon to mix together until well incorporated. There is no need to knead. Your dough will be like a wet, sticky scone dough, not like a regular bread dough.

2. Cover (but not airtight) and allow the dough to rest at room temperature until it rises (approximately 2 hours). You can use it immediately after the first rise, but the flavor is nicer if you refrigerate it in a lidded (not airtight) container overnight first.

3. Wet your hands and take a grapefruit-sized ball of the dough, quickly shaping it into a ball, gently pressing into shape and smoothing it with a little water if you don't want it to look rustic (I prefer the rustic look). Allow the dough to rest, loosely cover in plastic wrap on a small baking tray; sprinkled with polenta. Rest the dough for another 1.5–2 hours. It will rise a little in this time but not double in size.

4. 30 minutes prior to baking, preheat oven to 230°C (450°F), with a baking stone placed on the middle rack. Place an empty baking pan on the rack underneath.

5. When you loaf is ready to bake, use a very sharp knife or serrated bread knife to slash the top with shallow deep parallel cuts. Slide the loaf directly on to the hot stone. Quickly pour 250 ml (8½ fl oz) of hot water into the baking pan on the rack underneath and shut the oven door immediately.

6. Bake for 35–40 minutes, until lightly brown and firm. Allow your bread to cool on a wire rack before slicing and devouring. Sandwiches and toast will no longer be a distant memory.

MILLET, CHICKPEA *and* FETA SALAD
Serves 4

Sorghum is rich in iron, packed with magnesium and in this salad it's super crunchy, I love it!

INGREDIENTS

- 220 g (8 oz) hulled millet
- 1 tsp peanut oil
- 1 red onion, peeled and thinly sliced
- 1 x 400 g (14 oz) tinned chickpeas (garbanzo beans), drained and rinsed
- 40 g ($1^1/_2$ oz) dukkah
- 60 ml (2 fl oz) lemon juice
- 2 tbsp peanut oil, plus extra to serve

- 2 tsp mustard
- 2 tsp honey
- small handful baby spinach leaves
- 2 courgettes (zucchinis), shredded
- 100 g (4 oz) pepitas (pumpkin seeds)
- 20 g ($^3/_4$ oz) feta
- cilantro (coriander) leaves, to serve

METHOD

1. Bring a saucepan of boiling water to the boil over medium–high heat. Add the millet and cook for 5 minutes until tender. Strain and rinse under cold water and set aside.
2. Heat the oil in a large frying pan, add the onion and cook until softened. Add the chickpeas and dukkah and cook over a low heat until warmed through.
3. Place the lemon juice, oil and mustard and honey in a bowl and whisk to combine.
4. Place the spinach, chickpea mixture and millet in a large bowl and toss with the dressing.
5. Place the courgettes, pepitas and feta in a separate bowl and toss to combine.
6. Serve the millet mixture on top of the courgette and feta mixture and drizzle with extra oil and the cilantro leaves.

TAPIOCA FLOUR

Tapioca is the starch extracted from the cassava root. It's native to South America and has its origins in the north of Brazil. It's a staple food in many world regions and used as a thickening agent in many foods. It's one of the purest forms of starch foods. Tapioca pearls are often used in drinks, desserts, puddings and soups. They are produced by passing the moist starch through a sieve under pressure. It's often frowned upon as being extremely old fashioned and bland, which is a myth in my eyes as it's versatile and glue like. If you think about the pearls of tapioca a bit like some science atoms joining together to form a link, you can imagine the wide use of this flour when replacing standard plan (all-purpose) flour with tapioca flour. It's awesome with sweet recipes and its elastic qualities lend it to all kind of dishes. I remember my mother telling me about her boarding school days and the tapioca pearl milk desserts they used to serve up with caramelized brown sugar and apricots.

SPICED TAPIOCA PUDDINGS

Serves 6

My favorite spice blend is cinnamon, ginger, cloves and cardamom. All are rich and earthy, and in this pudding they are uplifted to addictive. Close your eyes and imagine you are in India. This makes the perfect encore to an amazing Indian feast. I would like to dedicate this recipe to the wonderful Indian women who work at Rowie's Cakes: their collective tireless efforts to produce an awesome product with a bucketload of love and smiles is something that makes my heart sing.

INGREDIENTS

- 500 ml (17 fl oz) almond milk
- 125 ml (4 fl oz) pouring cream
- 4 whole cloves
- 4 cardamom pods, lightly crushed
- ³/₄ tsp ground cinnamon, plus extra to serve
- ¹/₂ tsp ground ginger
- 70 g (2 oz) pearl tapioca
- 4 egg yolks
- 2¹/₂ tbsp good-quality honey

METHOD

1. Preheat oven to 160°C (320°F). Place 6 125 ml (4 fl oz) ramekins in a roasting pan or large ovenproof dish with enough boiling water to reach halfway up the sides of the ramekins. It's a good idea to place a wet, folded tea towel under the ramekins to prevent the bases cooking too quickly.

2. Combine the almond milk, cream and spices in a medium saucepan and bring just to a simmer over medium heat. In a small mixing bowl aerate your tapioca. Use a hand whisk to add the tapioca to the milk and cream mixture. Place over low heat and simmer gently, stirring, for 15 minutes or until the tapioca plumps up. Remove from heat and use a fork to remove the whole spices.

3. Use a hand whisk to whisk together the egg yolks and honey in a bowl until well combined. Gradually stir in the tapioca mixture until well combined. Divide the mixture evenly between your ramekins and sprinkle the tops with extra ground cinnamon.

4. Bake for 30 minutes or until the puddings are firm. You want the center of your puddings to be slightly soft in the center to the touch. Remove from the oven and allow the ramekins to cool on a wire rack for 5 minutes before serving.

BRAZILIAN CHEESE BREADS
Makes 15

Many years ago I used to sub-lease a factory three days a week where the other tenant used to make traditional Brazilian cheese breads. That "other" tenant was Alex Herbert, a talented and passionate chef who now runs the renowned Bird Cow Fish in Surry Hills. A This recipe is dedicated to Alex, and yes Alex; there is such a thing as an awesome Brazilian cheese bread.

INGREDIENTS

- 450 g (16 oz) tapioca flour
- 250 ml (8½ fl oz) milk
- 250 ml (8½ fl oz) vegetable oil
- 3 eggs
- 1 tsp salt
- 120 g (9½ oz) grated Parmesan

METHOD

1. Preheat oven to 180°C (350°F). Place all the ingredients in a food processor and blend until smooth. Grease 12 holes from two 12-hole muffin pans. Divide the mixture between the holes until each is three-quarters filled.
2. Bake for 20 minutes or until golden and cooked through, making sure that the trays are in the middle of the oven; if not, swap the trays halfway through baking).
3. Serve warm.

CASSAVA CAKE
Serves 12

Buy grated cassava from your gourmet greengrocer or ask them to order it in for you. Cassava is exotic to work with and a Filipino classic. It's springy and elastic in texture and easy to make. If you are stuck for cassava seek out your nearest traditional Asian grocer for some pre-grated frozen cassava and defrost before using. You are going to love this cake and, pretty please, do not be frightened about trying something different. The caramel with the cassava is an amazing combination and will send your guests to dessert heaven.

INGREDIENTS

- 900 g (2 lb) grated cassava
- 3 eggs
- 440 g (15¹/₂ oz) superfine (caster) sugar
- 190 ml (6¹/₂ fl oz) evaporated milk
- 310 ml (6¹/₂ fl oz) coconut milk
- 60 g (2 oz) unsalted butter, melted

Caramel topping
- 2 tbsp tapioca flour
- 400 g (14 oz) condensed milk
- 80 ml (2¹/₂ fl oz) coconut milk
- 2 egg yolks

METHOD

1. Preheat oven to 180°C (350°F). Grease and line a high-sided 22 x 7 cm (9 x 3 in) ovenproof dish.
2. Place all the ingredients (apart from the topping) in a mixing bowl. Use electric beaters to beat until well combined. Pour into the prepared dish and bake for 1 hour or until a skewer placed in the center comes out clean. Remove from the oven and allow to slightly cool.
3. For the topping, place the tapioca flour and half the condensed milk in a saucepan over heat and stir gently to combine. Add the coconut milk and the remaining condensed milk and cook over low heat for 10–15 minutes, stirring constantly until thickened. Remove from the heat.
4. Whisk your egg yolks in a bowl and stir in to the condensed milk mixture until well combined. Pour the topping over the warm cake. Use a kitchen blowtorch to golden the topping until caramelized. If you haven't got a blowtorch, place under a grill (broiler) preheated to a high heat for 3–5 minutes. Be very careful as it will caramelize quickly. Set aside at room temperature until the topping is set and your cake is completely cool.
5. Serve with mango, raspberries or a blackberries or mulberries.

INDIVIDUAL PAVLOVAS

Serves 6

The secret to the perfect pavlova is knowing your oven. Imagine your oven as a kiln firing up to bake earthenware—you are after crunch on the outside with softness in the center. It may seem odd to add tapioca flour but once you bake these classics you will never go back to any other method.

INGREDIENTS

- 4 egg whites
- 220 g (8 oz) superfine (caster) sugar
- 1 tsp white vinegar
- 1 tsp tapioca flour
- cream and berries, to serve

METHOD

1. Preheat oven to 180°C (350°F). Use electric beaters to beat the egg whites until soft peaks form, add $1/3$ of the sugar and beat for 3 minutes. Add half of the remaining sugar and beat for 5 minutes until the sugar dissolves, then add the remaining sugar and beat for a further 5 minutes or until sugar dissolves.
2. Fold in the vinegar and tapioca flour and mix well while keeping the air in the meringue.
3. Dollop the mixture, 4 cm (1½ in) apart, on a large, lined baking tray—you will have six pavlovas.
4. Place in oven, immediately reduce heat to 150°C (300°F) and bake for 50 minutes, or until dry and crunchy.
5. Turn oven off and leave to cool with the oven door ajar. Serve with cream and seasonal berries.

✖

TEFF

Step aside quinoa. Is teff the new superfood grain? Teff is from Ethiopia and is the smallest grain in the world, tinier than even the poppy seed. But it ticks many of the health boxes with an awesome fat profile, high mineral content, iron and calcium and is packed with vitamin B, so it's wicked for blood sugar management and gastro health as well as being gluten-free. Teff is similar to quinoa in terms of carbohydrate and protein content. Teff is also good for bone health because unlike a lot of other 'superfood' grains and seeds it contains vitamin K. When cooked, it works like polenta or semolina gruel and is perfect for soaking up sauces and being used as a porridge. Toasted and raw in a salad, it's awesome, but the most amazing thing is it how it perfoms as a flour. Due to its small size, the milling process is not thorough enough to remove any of the bran or germ, so all the nutrients are retained. It's a very exciting grain.

CINNAMON, COCONUT *and* TEFF PORRIDGE
Serves 4

Breakfast is a big thing for me. This one packs an amazing power punch and is perfect nutrition wise. Take the time to make it and then it will take the time to make your body happy. Give your mind some space to make this in the morning. You so deserve it. Sundays are on my mind.

INGREDIENTS

- 170 g (6 oz) teff flour
- 750 ml (26 fl oz) water
- 340 ml (12 fl oz) coconut milk
- 1 cinnamon stick
- 40 g (1½ oz) diced dates
- 55 g (2 oz) walnuts, chopped
- 2 tsp honey
- pinch of salt

To serve
- 1 banana, sliced
- blueberries
- extra diced dates

METHOD

1. Place the teff flour and water in a saucepan over high heat. Cover, bring to the boil then reduce heat to low and simmer for 10–15 minutes.
2. In a separate saucepan over low heat, bring the coconut milk, cinnamon stick and dates to a gentle simmer for 5 minutes.
3. Strain the cinnamon stick and dates, reserving the dates, and gradually add the flavored milk to the teff porridge, stirring, to get your favorite porridge consistency over medium heat.
4. Dry fry the walnuts in a small frying pan over medium heat for 1–2 minutes or until they start to char and smell nutty. Remove from heat and add the honey. Transfer to a lined baking tray, sprinkle with the salt and allow to cool.
5. Serve this wicked porridge in bowls topped with banana, walnuts, reserved dates and extra dates. Welcome to a beautiful day!

BANANA, COCONUT *and* CHERRY CAKES
Makes 12

I don't like the old-fashioned word muffin, so I am calling these little guys 'cakes'. Feel free to replace the cherries and bananas with other fruit.

―――――――――――――――――――――

INGREDIENTS

- 1 tbsp linseed
- 40 g (1½ oz) shredded coconut
- 125 g (4 oz) sugar
- 70 g (2½ oz) coconut oil
- 4 eggs
- 55 g (2 oz) coconut flour

- 55 g (2 oz) teff flour
- 2 tsp gluten-free baking powder
- 55 g (2 fl oz) vanilla yogurt
- 3 ripe bananas, mashed
- 100 g (3½ oz) frozen cherries, roughly chopped

METHOD

1. Preheat oven to 180°C (350°F). Line a 12-hole muffin tray with patty cases.
2. Combine the linseed, half the shredded coconut and 1 tablespoon of the sugar in a mixing bowl. Set aside.
3. Mix the coconut oil and remaining sugar until well combined. Beat in 2 of the eggs then half of the coconut flour. Mix well to ensure it's all combined before adding the remaining eggs, beating well between each addition, and the remaining coconut flour. Add the teff flour, baking powder, yogurt, banana and cherries to your batter and stir to combine well.
4. Divide the mixture between patty cases and sprinkle the reserved coconut mixture evenly on top. Bake for 25–30 minutes or until they are firm or a skewer inserted in the center of one cake come out clean. Transfer to a wire rack to cool. Store in an airtight container for up to 5 days. These are great lunch box treats!

HERBIE CHICKEN *and* TEFF MEATBALLS
Makes 4 Meatballs

INGREDIENTS

- 500 g (18 oz) chicken thigh fillets
- 2 fennel bulbs, sliced (fronds removed)
- 3 dill sprigs, finely chopped
- 3 parsley stalks, finely chopped
- 170 g (6 oz) teff flour
- 500 ml (17 fl oz) water
- 2 tsp smoky paprika
- 500 ml (17 fl oz) chicken stock
- 1 tbsp olive oil

- 1 brown onion, peeled and sliced
- 2 garlic cloves, peeled and crushed
- 70 g (2½ oz) button mushrooms, trimmed and sliced
- sea salt and freshly ground black pepper
- 1 tbsp ground turmeric
- 2 tsp ground cumin
- ½ lemon, zested and juiced
- sprinkle of fresh cilantro (coriander) leaves, chopped
- 250 ml (8½ fl oz) plain yogurt

METHOD

1. Place the chicken, fennel, dill, parsley and a pinch each of salt and pepper in a food processor and pulse until combined.

2. Roll golf ball sized meatballs, dipping your hands in cold water in between. Transfer your balls in to the fridge for 20 minutes to firm up.

3. In a medium saucepan, combine the teff flour, water, a pinch of sea salt, the paprika and 250 ml (8½ fl oz) of the stock. Cover with a lid place over high heat. Bring to the boil then reduce heat and simmer for 12–15 minutes. Set aside.

4. Add half the oil to a frying pan over medium–high heat and cook the meatballs for 3–5 minutes or until they are golden brown all over. Transfer to a plate lined with paper towel. In the same frying pan add the remaining oil and caramelize the onion over medium heat until golden brown. Add the garlic and stir for another minute, then add the mushrooms and sliced fennel and stir for another 3–5 minutes.

5. Add the cooked teff to the pan, sprinkle in the turmeric and cumin and season with salt and pepper. Deglaze the pan with the remaining stock and pop your gorgeous meatballs back in. Cover, reduce heat to very low and simmer for 10 minutes. Squeeze over the lemon, top with coriander and serve with a dollop of yogurt and lemon zest.

BAKED POTATOES *with* CHILI *and* ANCHOVIES
Serves 6

Teff, or the "grass of love", has an amazing calcium content. Outrageously, a cup of cooked teff gives you the same amount of calcium as a cup of cooked spinach. Beat that Popeye!

INGREDIENTS

- 1 kg (2 lb) potatoes, peeled and sliced
- sea salt and freshly ground black pepper
- 12 anchovy fillets
- 4 garlic cloves, peeled and chopped
- 2 red chilies, chopped
- ¼ bunch of sage leaves
- 3 bay leaves
- 40 g (1½ oz) teff flour
- 350 ml (11 fl oz) coconut cream
- 50 g (1 1/2 oz) butter, chopped

METHOD

1. Preheat oven to 180°C (350°F). Place the potato slices in a baking dish and season with salt and pepper. Sprinkle with anchovies, garlic, chili, sage and bay leaves.
2. Whisk the teff flour into the coconut cream and drizzle over the potatoes. Dot with butter, then bake for 1 hour.
3. Serve immediately.

MOLTEN CHOCOLATE PUDDINGS
Serves 4

These chocolate puddings are masters of seduction. They are like many gorgeous things in life and were probably discovered by accident. Timing is crucial so please take care when making these molten masterpieces.

INGREDIENTS

- *175 g (6 oz) dark chocolate, broken into pieces*
- *2 tbsp unsalted butter*
- *75 g (3 oz) superfine (caster) sugar*
- *2 eggs*
- *½ teaspoon vanilla extract*
- *sea salt*
- *2 tbsp teff flour*

METHOD

1. Preheat oven to 200°C (300°F). Place a baking tray in the oven until warm. Grease four dariole moulds and line the bases with discs of baking paper.
2. Melt the chocolate pieces in a bowl set over simmering water (make sure the base of the bowl doesn't touch the water), then remove from heat and set aside to cool slightly.
3. Use electric beaters to cream the butter and sugar until pale and fluffy. Beat in the eggs, one at a time, beating well between each addition, then add the vanilla and the salt.
4. Fold in the flour until just combined and gently mix in the cooled chocolate.
5. Divide the mixture between the moulds, place on the warm baking tray and bake for 8 minutes.
6. Turn out and serve immediately.

ROWIE'S GLUTEN-FREE PLAIN (ALL-PURPOSE) FLOUR MIX

Makes 3 lb (1.4 kg)

Easy and economical as you can blend this plain flour mix and store in an airtight container in your pantry for up to 3 months. I like to combine gluten-free flours, with different textures and different properties as it delivers a more versatile, gluten-free plain flour that you can substitute measure for measure in wheat flour-based recipes; and this base recipe is it. The properties of these three flours also mean you don't need to add gums to make your flours work together and hold when baked as they have gelatinous and glutinous pearly like properties which allow them to stand on their own.

INGREDIENTS

- 900 g (2 lb) rice flour (fine white rice flour; which can be found in Asian supermarkets or the international section of your local supermarket)
- 340 g (12 oz) of potato starch
- 150 g (5 oz) of gluten-free cornflour (cornstarch)

METHOD

1. Place all of the flours in a large mixing bowl and mix with a large whisk to combine. Alternatively, mix in a stand mixer on a low speed for 30 seconds. These will store in an airtight container in your pantry for up to three months.

TIP

Place a small portion of any different flour in a vessel and add a small amount of water to each; let it sit for 3 minutes and then touch with your finger or tap with a spoon and think about how it's reacted to the water and then think about those properties and what you can use the flours for. I loved researching this when I started my business; and I do love working like now as well—getting in touch with your inner professor is quite a godsend when experimenting with gluten-free baking! Happy Days!

ACKNOWLEDGEMENTS

A big thank you to Linda and Fiona for believing in me and *The Power of Flour*.

To Jessica from New Holland Publishers; thank you for your patience.

To Vicky, Roger, Cara and Gerri; lots of love and thanks.

Also; to Jason, Gerri and Bryan, Angelo, Matt, Kylie and Michelle thanks for giving me a break and an opportunity.

To my customers and suppliers; you know who you are and you are all my friends; I appreciate working with you every day. Thank you for being a massive part of the growth of my brand and my business.

To my team; all of you; throughout the years; a big, big thank you for being part of my business and my journey; I will be forever grateful for your hard work, generous time and for your love of what we do.

To all my family; I love you and thank you.

To all my special little friends that unlock the inner child in me; thanks for loving baking and cooking and thank you for your gorgeous pictures, cuddles, notes and menus and for making me laugh, smile and create! I love children and I wish I had my own; but none-the-less and even far greater; I am proud and honoured to have Audrey, Gracie, Olivia, Scarlett, Olivia, Bridget and Alice in my life. You make each day lighter and brighter.

To my gorgeous friends; you inspire me to inspire others; thank you.

To Andrew and Miranda and Shirley; thank you for your support and for having faith in my ability and creativity.

To all of you who have eaten your way through this book and it's many chapters; thank you.

And finally to Sue and Imogene; it's that moment when you stop at the end and say; "well that was an amazing creative journey; I'm absolutely honoured"; thank you for that generous moment in time.

Thank you also to the following for their generosity; help and support in the creation of my book: The gorgeous Georgie at Major and Tom for the rockstar cake stand, the unflappable Roger and team from Sheldon and Hammond for all the gorgeous International Bakeware, Scanpan, Cuisinart and Boards for backgrounds, to Ann Kidd and the wonderful team at Smeg Australia, to Toni and Guy hairdressing for always ensuring I look fabulous and finally to my Mum; I am sure I wouldn't be as creative as I am if I wasn't your daughter. Thank you.

AUTHOR BIOGRAPHY

Rowie Dillon is the Queen of gluten-free cooking. She has a passion for great food, culinary design and is protective about her diet. As an experimental cook, Rowie investigated ways of dealing with her body's digestive intolerances.

So in 2001 she created Rowie's Cakes— a kitchen where every wickedly delicious morsel that leaves the kitchen is 100% wheat free, dairy free and gluten free. Her range of products is testament to the fact that it is possible for naughty tasting food to be good for you.

Rowie has baked for Ellen De Generes, Cate Blanchett, Mick Jagger, Gerri Halliwell, the movie The Great Gatsby, Baz Luhrmann, Nicole Kidman, Tobey Macquire, Gerald Butler and many other celebrities and notaries.

Rowie also gives her time generously, supporting "Kids in the Kitchen" classes to help children gain a better and more fun understanding of Good Food Habits and supports events with Diabetes NSW and Equal.

As a pioneer in her field, Rowie is enthusiastic and passionate about food innovation and technique and making a difference.

Written by some of the gorgeous kids in my life

INDEX

First published in 2016 by New Holland Publishers Pty Ltd
London · Sydney · Auckland

The Chandlery Unit 704 50 Westminster Bridge Road London SE1 7QY United Kingdom
1/66 Gibbes Street Chatswood NSW 2067 Australia
5/39 Woodside Ave Northcote, Auckland 0627 New Zealand

www.newhollandpublishers.com

A record of this book is held at the British Library and the National Library of Australia.

ISBN: 9781742578132

Managing Director: Fiona Schultz
Publisher: Linda Williams
Project Editor: Jessica McNamara
Designer: Andrew Quinlan
Photographer: Sue Stubbs
Food Stylist: Imogene Roache
Production Director: James Mills-Hicks
Printer: Toppan Leefung Printing Limited

10 9 8 7 6 5 4 3 2 1

Keep up with New Holland Publishers on Facebook
www.facebook.com/NewHollandPublishers